The Four Questions of Melancholy

The Four Questions of Melancholy
New and Selected Poems

Tomaž Šalamun

edited by
Christopher Merrill

WHITE PINE PRESS • BUFFALO, NEW YORK

Translations ©1997, 2999, 2002, 2007 by Christopher Merrill, Michael Biggins, Sonja Kravanja, Charles Simic, Anselm Hollo, Elliot Anderson, Bob Perelman, Michael Waltuch, Michael Scammell, Veno Taufer, Deborah Kohloss, Mia Dintinjana, and Tom Lozar.

Acknowledgments: Grateful acknowledgment is made to the editors of the following journals, in which many of the newer poems were first published: *Agni, American Poetry Review, Boulevard, Cimarron Review, City Lights, Colorado Review, Denver Quarterly, Exquisite Corpse, Ironwood, Mississippi Review, New England Review/Bread Loaf Quarterly, New Letters, Nimrod, Paris Review, Partisan Review, Ploughshares, Poetry Miscellany, Trafika, Verse,* and *Willow Springs.*

Selections from *The Selected Poems of Tomaž Šalamun,* edited by Charles Simic. (New York: The Ecco Press, 1988). Reprinted by permission.

Selections from *The Shepherd, The Hunter* by Tomaž Šalamun, selected and translated by Sonja Kravanja. (Santa Fe: Pedernal Press, 1992). Reprinted by permission.

Epigraph from *The Poetry of Michaelangelo,* an annotated translation. Jane M. Saslow, Yale University Press, New Haven and London. Copyright 1991 Yale University.

Publication of this book was made possible, in part, by grants from the National Endowment for the Arts and the New York State Council on the Arts. Additional funding was provided by the Slovenian Ministry of Culture.

Cover art ©1997, 1999, 2002, 2007 by Metka Krašovec.

Printed and bound in the United States of America.

ISBN 978-1-877727-57-3

Fifth Edition

Terra Incognita Series, Volume I. Series General Editor: Aleš Debeljak

Published by White Pine Press, P.O. Box 236, Buffalo, New York 14201
www.whitepine.org

For Ana and David

Contents

Introduction

They are, of course, unanswerable, the four questions of melancholy at the heart of Tomaž Šalamun's poetry. Nor should we look to him—or any poet—for answers. Indeed, the memorability of a poem often depends upon the grace with which it articulates questions central to our experience. It was Rilke, after all, who advised a young poet "to try to love the *questions themselves* like locked rooms and like books that are written in a very foreign tongue." Such a discipline is central to Šalamun, whose poems—written in Slovenian, a language spoken by only two million people—open onto rooms filled with treasure, intimate truths of the human condition.

But why are the questions melancholy? Šalamun himself is blessed with an audacious poetic vision—"I was born in a wheat field snapping my fingers," he writes—and his work, at once improvisational and surreal, is nothing if not playful, like the very medium of language, which expresses itself most directly in poetry and jokes. Slovenian humor even marks that connection: if there are three Slovenians in a room, runs a popular joke, chances are all three are poets. For Slovenia, which until 1991 was the northernmost republic of Yugoslavia, is a country of poets: its public monuments commemorate bards, not military heroes; many of its Partisan brigades in World War II were named after writers; its new banknotes feature likenesses of Slovenia's most famous literary figures, France Prešeren and Ivan Cankar. Of his republic's declaration of independence from Yugoslavia in June 1991, which precipitated the savage Third Balkan War, the poet Aleš Debeljak suggests that it "literally meant the birth of a Slovenian nation-state from the spirit of poetry."

A difficult birth, then, after a long gestation. And if Slovenia has a national disease, it is melancholia—a legacy, perhaps, of more than a thousand years of subjugation to the whims of stronger powers. Franks, Bavarians, Hungarians, Teutons, and the Austro-Hungarian Empire, all ruled at one time or another over this tiny land wedged between the Julian Alps and the Adriatic Sea. "In the absence of a nation-state of their own," Debeljak notes, "the only real home for Slovenians was carved out in their language and poetry." Despite enormous pressure, political and cultural, to abandon their identity, the Slovenians created a rich and melancholic poetic tradition, which for much of their history united them as strongly as their Roman Catholic faith. Surely one sign of this people's impending change of fortunes was the appearance, in 1964, of a poet determined to upend that tradition. Nothing would ever be quite the same after Tomaž Šalamun published these lines:

> I grew tired of the image of my tribe
> and moved out.
>
> Out of long nails
> I weld limbs for my new body.
> Out of old rags, my entrails.
> A coat of carrion
> will be my coat of solitude.
> I pluck my eye from the depths of the marsh.
> Out of the devoured plates of disgust
> I will build my hut.
>
> My world will be a world of sharp edges.
> Cruel and eternal.

Slovenian poets and writers were not alone in recognizing Šalamun's originality. When the young poet was named editor of *Perspektive,* the republic's leading cultural and policical monthly journal, the Communist authorities banned its publication and arrested Šalamun, threatening him with a twelve-year prison sentence. Upon his release from jail five days later, thanks to international pressure, he was a cultural hero, a position reinforced by the *samizdat* publication of his first book, *Poker.* "Jail did me a great service," he writes in characteristically buoyant fashion, "since public attention focused on my poems and therefore I felt obliged to give my poetry everything in order to justify my unearned fame."

Who was this poet singlehandedly reshaping Yugoslavia's literary landscape?

The son of a pediatrician and an art historian, Tomaž Šalamun was born in Zagreb, Croatia in 1941. An infamous year. The zeal with which Croatia's pro-Nazi Ustaša regime, installed in April and bent on building an ethnically pure state, murdered Serbs, Jews, Gypsies, and other Croats alarmed even the German and Italian authorities, to say nothing of the citizenry. When Šalamun's father, a leftist sympathizer, learned from Jewish friends that his name was on the list of those to be liquidated, the family fled to Ljubljana, Slovenia, then under Italian control. The poet's first memory, in fact, is of an Italian soldier jumping on a roadblock, celebrating Italy's capitulation in 1943. The bombardments he experienced during the war, which he viewed as "a festival of light and particular energies," would resurface in the dark and explosive imagery of his first poems.

His family moved to Koper, a small town just south of Trieste; and after the war, when Trieste and the Istrian peninsula were divided into two zones, A and B, Šalamun came of age in the border area between the Eastern Bloc and the West—in Zone B, that is, which was run by the Yugoslav Army and which surrounded the Free Territory of Trieste, under American rule until 1954. Koper was Italian (Capodistria) before the partition, and even as a child the poet felt like an intruder in "this peaceful, Mediterranean, dreamy, old-time small town." Travels during his high school years to Brussels, Amsterdam, and Paris enlarged his understanding of the differences between the East and West, while the brilliant light along the Adriatic coast, which colored his imagination, gave him a new aesthetic orientation. If Vienna is the traditional lodestar of Slovenian poetry (as well as of its politics and culture), Šalamun looked for inspiration to Venice—and points further west.

Nor was this an act of revolt. His "is a poetics not of rebellion but of quest," Robert Hass explains. "Šalamun's tradition has been the disruptive, visionary side of European experimental art, Rimbaud, Lautréamont, the German expressionists, the French surrealists, the Russian futurists, the tradition in which poetry is an instrument for glimpsing a supreme reality, and for which all art is, finally, the scattered bits and pieces of that larger vision."

Šalamun's quest, which began at the University of Ljubljana, where he earned an M.A. in art history, took him to Paris and Rome for additional studies. Then he worked as an assistant curator at Moderna Galerija, Slovenia's modern art museum, and he was a conceptual artist affiliated with OHO, an avant-garde group which exhibited all over Yugoslavia and which was included in a show at the Museum of Modern Art in 1970. His first trip to New York convinced him to return to the city as a poet, not an artist, and on his subsequent journeys to the United States—as a member of the International Writing Program at the University of Iowa, as a resident of the Yaddo and McDowell writing colonies, and as a Fulbright Fellow—he wrote an astonishing amount of poetry. The poets of the New York School, particularly Frank O'Hara and John Ashbery, offered him a way out of Slovenia's strictures. America's open spaces, he once said, "open up my cells."

Nevertheless he could not escape his destiny in the Balkans. "The history of Slavs is, for example,/ utterly miserable," Šalamun reminds us. "Some small nations biting/ each other, because the weather is bad." That bad weather helps to explain what Hass rightly calls the "denser shadows" of the poet's work in the past fifteen years. With Tito's death in 1980 the whole of Yugoslavia suffered a darkening of the spirit—or should I say a truer accounting? Just as the Kingdom of Serbs, Croats, and Slovenes cobbled together in the wake of World War I did not survive the Nazi invasion, so Tito's Yugoslavia—literally, Land of the South Slavs—forged in the fires of World War II could not withstand the rising tide of nationalism. "Here is something we can all count on," writes Charles Simic. "Sooner or later our tribe always comes to ask us to agree to murder."

This was a summons Šalamun refused, replacing an outdated image of his tribe with a spirit of play, a counterweight to the dogmas of the ideologues—the blinkered and the blind. "Every true poet is a monster," he declares in "Folk Song." "He destroys people and their speech." By monster Šalamun means a force of nature, premonitory and divine, which unsettles expectations and beliefs, the cultural or tribal status quo, in order to restore to the individual a measure of worth. He himself is such a monster, he tells us in "History," as well as "a sphere rushing through the air." Perhaps this is what Simic means when he writes, "The lyric poet is almost by definition a traitor to his own people. He is the stranger who speaks the harsh truth that only individual lives are unique and therefore sacred. He may be loved by his people, but his example is also the one to be warned against. The tribe must pull together to face the invading enemy while the lyric poet sits talking to the skull in the graveyard." This is the sort of talk dear to Šalamun. "Only the poet sells his soul to separate it/ from the body that he loves," he writes. And what remains is sacred.

18

The four questions of melancholy, like the four directions of the wind, change with each telling. Hence the sheer variety of forms Šalamun employs. Here are surrealist lists, Whitmanic catalogues, sonnets, New York School-style improvisations. "Poetry is a parallel process to spiritual development," he said in an interview. "As in religion, you are trained not to be scared. As in the cabala or in dervish dances, you are trained how to be with the world as long as you can endure it." And what is remarkable about Šalamun is his willingness to follow the language to the border beyond which lie madness and suicide. "Why does the thread hold together?" he asks in "Are Angels Green?" Because, as he has discovered, sometimes language behaves "like a dolphin, it is pure grace, you just follow grace, and you have this feeling of water and light."

The Four Questions of Melancholy brings together poems from each of Šalamun's twenty-five volumes published in Slovenia. Building on The Selected Poems of Tomaž Šalamun, handsomely edited by Charles Simic and introduced by Robert Hass, this book includes a substantial selection of new work translated by Michael Biggins as well as poems from Šalamun's most recent collection, Ambergris, which was published in 1994. Of his newest poems it may be wise to recall Picasso's words: "I have not painted the war...but I have no doubt that the war...is in these paintings I have done." Šalamun does not directly address the war that destroyed the former Yugoslavia. Rather, his poems are imbued with the tragedy the world has watched on television these past years. And while these poems do not provide answers to any questions, readers will find their longings for truth posed in such an original fashion that for a moment it may seem as if the darkening world has taken on a musical cast, an imaginative hue.

–Christopher Merrill

The Four Questions of Melancholy.

I say that for one who lives, whatever dies
cannot appease desire; nor can the eternal
be sought in time, where human flesh still alters.
*   Unbridled desire is merely the senses, not love,*
and slays the soul; our love makes us perfect friends
down here, but even more, through death, in heaven.

—Michelangelo
Sonnet, ca. 1535-41,
for Tomaso de Cavalieri

Eclipse

I

I grew tired of the image of my tribe
and moved out.

Out of long nails
I weld limbs for my new body.
Out of old rags, my entrails.
A coat of carrion
will be my coat of solitude.
I pluck my eye from the depths of the marsh.
Out of the devoured plates of disgust
I will build my hut.

My world will be a world of sharp edges.
Cruel and eternal.

II

I will take nails,
long nails
and hammer them into my body.
Very very gently,
very very slowly,
so it will last longer.
I will draw up a precise plan.
I will upholster myself every day
say two square inches for instance.

Then I will set fire to everything.
It will burn for a long time,
it will burn for seven days.
Only the nails will remain,

all welded together and rusty.
So I will remain.
So I will survive everything.

III

In the black meadows
hang the tarpaulins of my drying love.

No one is allowed on my land.

You never
walked on my grass,
don't ever think you did.
Only on the wall.
On top of the wall.
On the bottom of the wall.
On the left side of the wall.
On the right side of the wall.

Only on the wall.

Responsibility

Have you ever seen God
running so he'll make it by two-thirty
responsibility responsibility
approaching neither start nor finish
immovable attached
instead of just dangling its legs
responsibility responsibility
world without nature
world without discourse
trees, while still growing, are not responsible
and what is the word supposed to do with it
the sun doesn't need it for setting
nor the sky which is sheer blueness and nothing more
in the beginning there was transparency
a world of things and true language
words were things
things were words
who did God consult
when he made a butterfly as it is
when he could have made its legs six inches thick
responsibility responsibility
baroque sustenance of the people

The Arm

One day you realize that your arm
which after all is used to being an arm
has become inflated with its arm-ness
it looks at you dimly, used to being an arm
but what now and what will be the consequences
wildly you cast off what isn't yours
and ask why do you have to be an arm
be sand or water
or the transition from light to darkness
don't like it says the arm, you've been ignorant too long
not you I am the arm
but what now and what will be the consequences
who will establish the new boundaries
you've misunderstood says the arm
not you I am the arm, expanding
then I am a shoulder
I'm pale and I sing, sing loudly
and make the bed
let up for once with your petty jaundiced thoughts
you're not pale, you didn't sing, you didn't sing out loud
or make the bed
not you I am the arm
the world is the end of the world
but what now and what will be the consequences

The Cross

I'll draw a cross

serpentines on my rocking chair
how pathetically the shirt hangs
once the body leaves it
yet it's still a shirt
and here's what clinches our defeat
both a suitcase and a T-bar
have you ever seen a chair
running from the bathroom toward the kitchen
or vice-versa it doesn't matter
hysterically asking
what about my eternal life
have you ever seen a balcony railing
saying I've had enough
I've had enough
I've had enough
I too am fond of my modest life
I too must have my share
and if you've walked down Glagoljaška Street
and seen an old boot lying
between house number four and the well
left there from that year when
the last nighttime regattas took place and Mario won
did the boot ask you
hello excuse me
for bothering you here on the street but
doesn't it seem to you
doesn't it seem to you
doesn't it seem to you

things are inscrutable in their craftiness
unattainable to the rage of the living
invulnerable in their endless flight
you can't catch up with them
you can't seize them
motionless in their gaze

Homage to Hat & Uncle Guido & Eliot

Just like Clay who became a world champion
because there was something wrong with his leg
I'll be a great poet
because they screwed me up
with Frank's blue cap
sent for Christmas 1946
and since then I've left him out of my prayers
song of songs of the Pan-Šalamunian religion
terribly democratic people's institution
which takes in everything
from stamps biscuits Tzilka, Horak, Parmesan
to that poor idiot
who drank his hotel away in Ventimiglia
and faded out somewhere in the world
just as our prayer fades out
its last important reformer was Uncle Guido
known among the people
for his invention of a new pipe for the steam boiler
but that was not his main occupation
his main thing was
watering flowers
just like Spinoza
a bit taller though
meditating on and off on death
buying us ice cream
made fresh every day

that was between
magnolia Brandenburg & America

two days ago Eliot died
my teacher

Peace to the People of This Earth

God remembers all the travelers
           remembers rain in Arras
           and David's son
remembers a squirrel falling on the earth
           I yell rabbits
thinking they were really rabbits because I'm short-sighted
                     God remembers Stavrogin
remembers churn of rotten wood and our games
           the way I clean my teeth
                and say peace to the people of this earth
out of all the Empire-style furniture
           I like Napoleonic legs
                God remembers
                God remembers how painstakingly I worked
           to make a tetrahedron out of a slice of bread
and kept throwing it furiously against the wall
                and there was the war
                and parents saved sugar
The fire is getting closer
              night or whiskers
I see hell where my angel used to stand

Pity

On the subject of god briefly
he never said very much
never said rosemary
never said peace-loving
if there were ants in the corners
the ants stayed in the corners

for example dust
wherever it falls
down or to the side
or the existence of roots
all that god solves expertly

at times he says ARCHAIC
but nobody budges
nobody wakes up
really nobody wakes up
at times he says we kill
those who bring flowers

and he buys light-colored paper
I bought light-colored paper
he says we killed those who brought flowers
and he commands the little boat to sail the sea
the trees to bend
something to fall so it creaks

you're the light of the world
no hiding place even in the mountains

Tea

tea knows precisely why it is tea
it has no desire to be Cataline
here he comes again that ancient one
how I used to sit in Bruges
in my brown gaberdine suit
and eat something similar to calamari
and my friend Sicco van Albada
son of the redheaded Jewess my father's friend
how he used to try to persuade me
incessantly go back go back to Beffroi
because I had left my knapsack there
staring at the Beguine sisters
the way they looked on the road
and at swans at the drowning of Memling Gruuthuus
at Christine interpreting the legend of St. Ursula
then all of a sudden a Mr. Content
Belgian gynecologist tells me
I used to know Marini personally what a failure
is that supposed to be a horse
and for the first time there was
this incredible creak in my lining

Vacation Time

I catch my grandfather basking in the sun
under the oleander or sitting very straight
the way he praises the beekeeper
or says when is lunch going to be ready
or eats his breakfast

he seals the envelope
addressed to the Commission for the Investigation of War Crimes
or simply sleeps
or points out the window and says cut that tree down
that tree   those are mosquitoes
and here comes Mrs. Abramič and we take the train
and we're in Brežice and Grandpa is nervous
and in Rogaška Slatina
and the horse chestnuts and the brass band
and Mrs. Senčar playing piano and us keeping time

and there are four of us
it will be hell to change trains
and Jelka is crying because she lost her green pebble
the most important one for the gateway to her little garden
and Tzilka steals some flowers
and someone is playing with a needle the needle bends
the weather is going to be ruined

Grandpa totally unconcerned
just keeps on reading
Flora und Fauna in den Alpen
Flora und Fauna in den Alpen
Flora und Fauna in den Alpen

[untitled]

one day in the dining room I took the exact measurements
of the distance from the lower left-hand corner of the picture to the
       floor
and the distance from the lower right-hand corner to the floor
as I had the persistent feeling that the picture was hanging
one day I realized there is a dolphin roe
one day I took the suspenders out of the closet
one day it said in the papers
the King of Cambodia would return our visit
one day I thought who'll be the first one to count up to a million
one day I went out in the street to get some exercise
I walked on the right-hand side of the sidewalk
one day it occurred to me that every human being has to die
one day M. France bought a grove of birch trees
from a young artist because it occurred to him
that you have to take risks to get into the money
one day I bought pretzels although that is something I never do
because the dust lies on the street
one day St. Arnolfina appeared on the calendar

Heracles

Now Heracles performed many more great labors
back there on the Peloponnesus
and then went to Aetolia, its capital city, Kalydon
ruled by King Oineos.
Now Oineos had a most desirable daughter, named Deianeira
whose multitudinous suitors were so persistent and forward
they made her miserable,
more miserable than any other girl in Aetolia.
Now she had been reared in Pleuron, the second city
and there Acheloos, the river god, had seen her and become
hideously infatuated! And thus
he kept appearing before her father
asking for permission to marry her—
1) in the ensorcelled flesh of a genuine bull
2) as a continually mutating dragon
and 3), and last, in human form, but with a steer's head
from which curly head poured rivulets of the clearest water.

[untitled]

if you grab a chicken by its feet
and by its wings and with a sudden movement
turn it on its back and at the same time
slowly press it against the table
it will stiffen in that unnatural position
drift into sleep its feet stretched out
without strength its talons trembling
occasionally and the chicken staying like that
as if tied to the table even if you were
to step aside imperceptibly the chicken
will remain ten or more minutes as if
spellbound

Proverbs

1. Tomaž Šalamun made the Party blink, tamed it, dismantled it, and
   reconstituted it.
2. Tomaž Šalamun said, Russians Get Out! and they did.
3. Tomaž Šalamun sleeps in the forest.

Let's Wait

what are you wearing
I'm wearing dark green pants of thin corduroy
black boots and a sweater
how do you feel about physics
I think physics is an extremely interesting science
and I could be a physicist if I felt like it
who's your girlfriend
Maruška Krese
what do you do with her
first I say to her Maruška baby Mummy's sweetiepie
then I kick her out because I have to work
then you don't know how to create harmony
between art and women
no
do you think that's the reason artists tend to be melancholic
that's possible
how is it all going to end
it will end in marriage
plenty of kids
why
because I'm a jew
what about homosexuality doesn't it puzzle you
no it puzzled me at first
I buried and moved out two very nice women
then I went to bed with a black man
where did this happen
in Rome
what was his name
Kirk
is that how you spent your government scholarship
that's it
a government scholarship well invested

[untitled]

I read about Borges, pasting posters on walls
in Buenos Aires. It makes me feel good.
I watch his bloodthirsty mother
in a movie. The way I drive identifies me

immediately as a European.
Barry Watten says: Your eyes turn
like a torpedo, when you park. Right!
Americans turn their eyes like humming-

birds and find a parking lot. Frank
O'Hara would rather be a painter. I
think I *am* a painter. I keep on laughing

or am melancholic as a monkey.
Actually, I'm such a Mediterranean rock
you can broil steak on me.

I Have a Horse

I have a horse. My horse has four legs.
I have a record player. On my record player I sleep.
I have a brother. My brother is a sculptor.
I have a coat. I have a coat to keep me warm.
I have a plant. I have a plant to have green in my room.
I have Maruška. I have Maruška because I love her.
I have matches. With matches I light cigarettes.
I have a body. With a body I do the most beautiful things that I do.
I have destruction. Destruction causes me many troubles.
I have night. Night comes to me through the window of my room.
I have fun racing cars. I race cars because car racing is fun.
I have money. With money I buy bread.
I have six really good poems. I hope I will write more of them.
I am twenty-seven years old. All these years have passed like
      lightning.
I am relatively courageous. With this courage I fight human stupidity.
I have a birthday March seventh. I hope March seventh will be a nice
      day.
I have a friend whose daughter's name is Breditza. In the evening
      when they put her to bed she says Šalamun and falls asleep.

Jonah

how does the sun set?
like snow
what color is the sea?
large
Jonah are you salty?
I'm salty
Jonah are you a flag?
I'm a flag
the fireflies rest now

what are stones like?
green
how do little dogs play?
like flowers
Jonah are you a fish?
I'm a fish
Jonah are you a sea urchin?
I'm a sea urchin
listen to the flow

Jonah is the roe running through the woods
Jonah is the mountain breathing
Jonah is all the houses
have you ever heard such a rainbow?
what is the dew like?
are you asleep?

Are Angels Green?

Are angels green? Can the sky support them?
Workers have a mouth, a face, a walk, kids
little lambs lick grass, tigers tear meat,
to get water they go down to the river.

I've seen the rainbow going down,
shepherds swimming over,
I waved, I waved, felt I was burning,
I knew I was awake, wondered who was singing.

Who made you, day? Where do ants come from?
Why does the thread hold together?
Why does daylight fall on the knife?
Stupid maturity, rubbing my collar.

Where are the blacksmiths to forge my shoes?
I don't like them to cover my eyes,
I want the light to strike me, air,
I want everyone to breathe, mouse, shit.

Silently Flutter the Angels

immortality, verbs of the sun,
stop, rest, lay the flutes aside,
I sail, I sail in the silent seed of animals
in the circles of turning, uprooted stick of night
a stone, Pan, mountains of evenness
ides of March, door to dawn
a thousand seas, ash of lava,
a thousand furrows of tranquility
I am dealt out, underfoot, great in tiny vermin's eyes
leaning back
O hot Israelite's hoof, carriage game
consistent denominators of even days
I call the water, I sacrifice the lamb
splendor of stable, green stone of blossoming
I fall in the lime of grace
who tears daisies, white blossoms of itch?
to whom does the raindrop fall?
joyfulness, wind, slate of light, sea of burden
wake up stable hands, in the name of god the day is coming
pick up fern
rest weary rivers, the avalanche flocks
I will kill you Israel
body of Gilgamesh set among flowers
Uruk, the bait, Indians on the rafts
targets, breasts, people's trinkets
bowels, pails, ruler of toll roads
silently flutter the angels, silently in the nets of stars
I won't be plucked, I won't kneel on the prints of trains
I won't be wakened by shepherds
I'll breathe light, I'll utter aims
the strength of body, I'll spread avalanche
hear flutes, plant a tree
let it be clear what the hands of the king are
clear the hill, clear the life
clear the path of the Milky Way, clear the gift

The Shadow

Night fell once you had forded the stream
my hands are clean, I dare not look up
or down at the water, death is glowing
the fires are dim, the air a verdant soot

at times I pick a rose, it lights upon your image
you laugh, I sit down on the pier
I hear oars rowing, malicious people
if only I could grow, if it would just start spinning

if only it would shine both night and day, day and night
if only it would rain, if only the light were dazzling
if only I could look and touch and scream
if only the ground would open up, if only the air were pure

if only I could feel your skin, your teeth, your waist
if only I were yours, could hold you once again and stroke you
could tell you fairy tales, breathe as you did
god, talk and breathe and laugh and be your shadow.

[untitled]

Lord, how I rise
how strong I am, terrible and wise
how I undress, peel and migrate
it's done by you god, I kill

there are flowers in the garden, the air walks into my mouth
there are butterflies in the desert, meat in mothers
if I put a watch around my wrist, I jubilate
drums, drums, steam flows, pours

blissful fuck sovereign, your food is ours
peach trees, bodies, mountains, smoke
the dead, their skin, necklaces
I pluck golden teeth, sell them for bread

angels stand up from the sea, cherubim flutter
my verses are like splitting rocks
crushing jaws and shouting, let me eat lord
let me be your supreme law all the way to the end

The Difference

Did you open his eyes? Did you think he was unfriendly?
I didn't open his eyes. I didn't think he was unfriendly.
Will you burn him? Will you bring him wings?
I won't burn him. I won't bring him wings.
What's his profession?
Driver. He drives in the dust all day.
Does he splash when the snow falls?
When the snow falls he clings to chains.
Where did you meet him?
In the woods. He said he wanted to be a pilot. He
wanted to know if it's much warmer down south
and if there's much difference between footprints.

Drums

I am the people's point of view, a cow,
the tropical wind, I sleep under the surface.
I am the aristocratic carnivore, I eat form.
I drum on cooks' white caps, I drum on their

aprons, I am the green integration, water flows
into the infirmary, there is ice on the boots
made of damp. Little drums, flooding Styx,
little snouts, a dog snarls in the picture.

A churned temperature, a door, I threw the gold
ring into the boiling oatmeal. Here is autumn,
destiny has the same sphere, pedestrians stink.
New snow falls on snowballs.

The meadow is soaked, scarlet coats,
the air whirls, the thicket whirls over the desert.
They beat carpets, the color gets up with the sunrise.
More people will see me, with sunrise I become morning.

Sunflower

I

Are you asleep, a sunflower, black seed, gold,
are you asleep, the gods spread their wings over you.
Black venom, a closed miracle,
are you asleep, the dew flattens you.

You sleep, you wake bewitched,
dust and whirlpools of trains, of field paths,
you are asleep and you are expecting a bride,
a black rain, drops of light.

A black sword, a sunflower, golden bondsman,
a poppy and a weed, the steps of tired people,
. their boats, loaded with soil, your death,   .
sister of the sun, a statue of greeting.

In the glow I meditate on my sins,
crickets, a red brick driven into the ground,
pumpkins, brothers, winged animals,
sunflower, we share the land, silence of turning.

II

Shouts are words, silent sleep,
shouts are the sky, from the mouth in the mountains.
Shouts are men like dust in the desert,
dark lambs, the clear mill.

Shouts are haughtiness, bandages of sand.
In the clear hour of the bell, the black career.
Shouts are a sovereign, abysses of men,
stones in the dust, Ron, the moss.

Like the green beasts in the grain of bread,
like the innocent asleep, the burden of valleys.
The magnificent horseshoes, the growth of the day,
cold marshes, glowing breeds.

Violent silent landslide, gestures in smoke,
owls, birds, knocking of anvils.
Dead bull-calves, dead Maria,
mountains crushed, harrows cast with earth.

III

Don't be afraid of images of the world,
child. Close your eyes. Don't be afraid
of roads, the dead in trees. Don't be afraid
of cries and valleys, look, the world doesn't

wither, the skin turns to coal. Don't be
afraid of meadows, the ones who died of plague,
don't be afraid of the ones wrapped in color,
irritated men. Mothers rot and come back,

angels sleep, blackness waits for you,
a white light. Don't be afraid of castles
made of sand around the house, of the ones
who protect against fire, of the ridges

of signs. You are eating blood off tin,
salt off the mane of a horse, you belong to
silence and animals, to pilgrims of the door.
Don't be afraid of towers, of fires

in the ranks, don't be afraid of miracles.
Cheers, you swim in lavishness. Wings
of starved tribes, shouts of dreams,
the guardian angel watches over your night.

IV

Reflect, children, glide silently.
Reflect, men, animals, reflect.
Reflect, tired ones, hills, reflect.
Colors, reflect, reflect upon blood.

Reflect the earth. Reflect, clear relations,
flowers and storms, passions and gloom.
Reflect, fire, longing, reflect.
Reflect pages, reflect upon the wind, reflect, messengers,

reflect upon names, paths and time,
reflect upon the dust, upon room in the house.
Reflect upon the trampling of hooves, upon brightness of plains,
reflect upon orders, upon voices of holy people.

Upon burdens of the guides, reflect, black seed,
upon stones under the weight of herons, reflect, fields.
Mountains and woods, reflect, white brothers,
reflect, reflect upon suffering, sleep.

Dead Men

dead men, dead men
where in the steppes the birds flit and the day splits in half
where the cube heads are sailboats of whispering and the wagon
        loads of boards rebound off cliffs
where mornings glitter like the eyes of Slavs
where in the north the beavers slap each other, it resounds as an
        invitation to death
where the children point to their livid eyes and jump with rage on
        the timber
where, with their torn-off arms, they scare the bulls belonging to the
        neighbors
where they stand in line for the cold
where the bread stinks of vinegar, women of wild animals
dead men, dead men
where the tusks flash and fairy tales rustle
where the highest art is to nail the slave in midair
where the corn is burned on the vast plains so that God can smell it
dead men, dead men
where there are special churches for birds to teach them to bear the
        burdens of their souls
where the inhabitants at every meal snap their braces and step on
        sacred texts under the table
where the little balls are orange, mothers are nailed onto square
        shapes
where the horses are black with soot
dead men, dead men
where the skittles are tools of giants bruising their greasy hands on
        logs
where Šalamun would be greeted with screams
dead men, dead men
where all doormen are yellow men because they blink faster
where meat dealers are beaten to death with rackets and left
        unburied

where the Danube flows into the movie, from the movie into the sea
where the soldier's bugle is the signal for spring
where souls leap high and whisper in chorus
dead men, dead men
where the reading is strengthened with gravel, to be heard when we
      strike it, it booms
where the trees have screw threads, the boulevards knee joints
where they cut into children's skin the first day after birth, as into
      cork trees
where they sell alcohol to the old women
where the youth scrapes his mouth as the dredger scrapes the
      bottom of the river
dead men, dead men
where mothers are proud and pluck out filaments from their sons
where the locomotives are covered with elk's blood
where the light rots and cracks
where the ministers are dressed in granite
where wizardry causes animals to fall into baskets, the jackals
      tread on the eyes of otters
dead men, dead men
where one marks the sides of the sky with the cross
where the wheat is rugged and the cheeks puffed up by fires
where the flocks have eyes of leather
where all waterfalls are of dough, they tie them with black ribbons of
      young beings
where they break the instep bones of geniuses with timber hooks
dead men, dead men
where photography is limited to plants that grow and blow up the
      paper
where the plums dry in the lofts and fall in the old songs
where soldiers' mothers wheel the food parcels up to the rack
where the herons are built as athletic Argonauts
dead men, dead men
where sailors come to visit
where in the villas the horses neigh, the travelers smell
where the little bathroom tiles are covered with drawings of iris seeds

where the cannibals are fed wooden shingles
where the vine branches are wrapped in gray veils so that the eyes of
        the jealous film over

Pirates and St. Francis

Pirates, St. Francis, it's time
to sleep, rest from our journey,
nihilists and herds, you lean back and
stretch out, too, shepherds protect us

Sins protect us, the wings of peaceful valleys
cliffs and springs, good earth and roots
ashes of gutted settlements, jealous dragonflies
masts of ships, rumble of mills

Pitched hay protect us, blue ruminant fish
pines, lone houses
archers protect us, dead livestock offered to gods
songs of our heretic brothers, wood spirits

Venus, protectress of thieves, whortleberries, deer
children's laughter, scullers in the Arno
market, Mafia, sailors scorched by sun protect us
the movements of animals lull us to sleep.

Red Flowers

Red flowers grow in the sky, there's a shadow in the garden.
The light penetrates, there's no light to be seen.
How then can the shadow be seen, there's a shadow in the garden,
all around big white stones lie scattered, we can sit on them.

The hills around are just like the hills on earth, only lower.
They look perfectly tender. I think we, too, are perfectly light,
we hardly touch the ground. When I take a step,
it seems the red flowers draw back a little.

The air is fragrant, both cool and burning. New beings
draw closer, some invisible hand smoothly placing them in the grass
They are beautiful and quiet. We are all here together.
Some of them, swimming toward this place

are turned around in the air and cut off.
They disappear, we can't see them anymore, they groan.
Now my body feels as if it's in a fiery tunnel,
it rises like dough, drizzles apart in the stars.

There is no sex in heaven, I feel no hands,
but all things and beings are perfectly joined.
They rush apart only to become even more united.
Colors evaporate, all sounds are like a sponge in the eyes.

Now I know, sometimes I was a rooster, sometimes a roe.
I know I had bullets in my body, they crumble away now.
How beautifully I breathe.
I feel I am being ironed, it doesn't burn at all.

Words

You catch water with a pin,
the water turns to slush.
You point at the tree with your hand,
the tree burns.
You divide lines with a shadow.
You open the door for love and death.

Who's Who

Tomaž Šalamun you are a genius
you are wonderful you are a joy to behold
you are great you are a giant
you are strong and powerful you are phenomenal
you are the greatest of all time
you are the king you are possessed of great wealth
you are a genius Tomaž Šalamun
in harmony with all creation we have to admit that
you are a lion the planets pay homage to you
the sun turns her face to you every day
you are just everything you are Mount Ararat
you are perennial you are the morning star
you are without beginning or end
you have no shadow or fear
you are the light you are the fire from heaven
behold the eyes of Tomaž Šalamun
behold the brilliant radiance of the sky
behold his arms behold his loins
behold him striding forth
behold him touching the ground
your skin bears the scent of nard
your hair is like solar dust
the stars are amazed who is amazed at the stars
the sea is blue who is the sky's guardian
you are the boat on high seas
that no wind no storm can destroy
you are the mountain rising from the plain
the lake in the desert
you are the *speculum humanae salvationis*
you hold back the forces of darkness
beside you every light grows dim
beside you every sun appears dark
every stone every house every crumb every mote of dust
every hair every blood every mountain every snow

every tree every life every valley every chasm
every enmity every lamb every glow every rainbow

I See

Hunters dressed in sunlight, I see roes with dogs,
lumps, bellies of bulls, a comet,
I see thorns and rattling chains, food in a column,
crunching gums, a day in the factory,
I see millstones, wax tablets,
bodies nailed up in a millet, I see horses and Split.
I see lorries and boards, birds, a chisel scattered in sky-blue,
castles and choir, I see whatever I touch,
I see honey, a plucking of centennial oaks,
beavers and arches, how four glistens.
I see the ardent faces of frightened men,
nobility's hush and midnight's guards, garret windows.
The desert where it is written: bus, salt,
basins, electricity of birds.
How lapis rustles, a drum skin, a *mbira,*
I see crushed chalk in the slaves' eyes, a mischief,
I see Zadar in Mally's hands, a shifting of the enemy,
sheep with shaved heads, a lamb in steam.
I see hail, old women in front of crosses,
a cartilage and a flood of black dough,
a tide of the unreasonable, a mob, watchmakers,
whitings, from which a housekeeper's fat strains
I see flax, the flax, thighs in exultation,
banners stabbed in llama backs,
churches crumbled into yellow pails.
I see how bristles turn up cats, how a palm twitches,
how bromine evaporates in the throats of madmen
I see a fat mestizo, a Greek whose flower tears,
I see corn, how the army goes after the scent of cantaloupe,
the night smells in Ca' Foscari.

Weight

I stroke the parchment and dream, darkness falls
a wild landslide buried the murmur of spruce
squirrels, so high up, so serene
along the mountain paths, the walls of changed days

the only ones, master, dark and glowing as lightning phantoms
pressed with the seal, Phaeton's fall
the arc of guiltless horses racing to earth
for some a gift, for others, manes grasped in flight

I live for this: to sink in the sun
to gaze at light like the level sea
to see the dust and in the dust a field
in eyes the lord's footsteps, a velvet silence

to fall as you see fit, without passion
you stranger, you silent night, my prey
to be a jackal on the prowl, ruined monster
beside you in fluttering summons, the weight of the law

I Am a Mason

I am a mason, a priest of dust
fortified like a monster, a crust of bread
I am a water lily, a soldier of holy trees
holy dreams, with the angels I shout

I am a castle, a dead rock wall
I carry the boats, a ferryman
O wood! wood!
come here, little herons, a seed

come, gardeners! light, appear!
come, spread hands, pane of glass
blue whirls, come, smooth plain
the wind, of the sliding, of creatures on different levels

the pastures are burnt, lava seething
shepherds are waiting, restless, trampling with their wings
dogs, smelling themselves, the wolf-dogs
here the memory stands, the order, the signs of the future

White Ithaka

salute me stars
set the fire, the nape of beasts
ignite the cold, arcadia
grape flames in shadow, a helmet's thud

show me the ocean, christening, greed,
white sheep straying, seared flesh
let me see color sailing
hear peals of our lady, fallen balustrades

let me give flight to creatures, bread to people
sin to soft breezes, a razor to wine
let me see ships of bauxite, sun in the earth
chains on the walls, a tribe of days

join forces stars, burn down in blueness
leave no scent no crumbs no silence no image
let me see bamboo, native fields
the chewing of deer, white Ithaka

[untitled]

One must cook well for one's husband and pigs.

I comb my daughter's hair.
Where are you going, stars?

For Ana

Ana grows.
Squirrels cavort.
I am at peace.
How can we know when it will truly collapse,
when the air will decant in a different form —
which must happen to us constantly, if we're to breathe —
and how to endure thinking we mustn't demand the miracle,
which is here, eternal, rarely attained,
sealed for our use.
How to crackle the package's paper and ribbons patiently,
humbly, attentively,
for within our range is everything and nothing more
than searching,
a laying on of lips.

I vanish, vanish, vanish
to husk moss,
to form a crust for two lenses,
two inventions in one.
No innovations.
Innovations must be aimed at the heart, which has always
been here, skidding in place.
If I am food, I'm as sated as a cat.

Hey, my regards to the Slovenians, and to your loved ones.
Tell them not to flap, everything is just and sufficient,
let it drip out as it will.
Maruška bakes homemade bread as we fly,
we upend the world, fall, pick ourselves up,
laugh like lunatics,
or we're boarded up tight like a cabin that burns
and never had a door.
Mostly we're happy and stand in the open.

I eat blue imagination till my throat bursts,
you eat blue imagination till your throat bursts,
he eats blue imagination till his throat bursts.
There's no time for shoving, pushing, despair,
there is only time for light and floating and holding on,
nothing perishes.

We eat this landscape in a different way, at a distance.
No need to sand the stomach walls of Logos from the inside
out, because it arrived in pieces and was never
really put together.
The parts were set out at intervals like gas pumps
and fields, hence no liquids
trapped in bottles here.
If you take a gallon on the road, you'll use up three
hundred gallons to California, you could even die of drought
if you had a thousand gallons in your tank. It vanishes.
You're infinitely smaller in this landscape. It hums.
The trees grow beneath a sky that's even round
ahead, beneath the earth. Death is a given.
Whoever doesn't have that mounted in his heart will freeze.
But there is also an unending generosity,
a multitude of lives that drop like cells from the mass
into and around us.
You are the same.
Know this:
jump into a farmhand's mouth and inhabit heaven.
It's for you.
The water seethes and rots and carries the boat.
Even so.
Even so radiates, not like *yes but,* which is scraggly,
dark and falters.
The ship breaks roof beams in the ocean.

Don't believe in *yes but,* which has cost us thirty percent
of all Slovenian lives.

The average loss is greater for small nations.
Small nations inhabit Europe like boils.
Throw the blood out, it comes rushing back.
The womb is collective and for everyone, like the manger
beneath a Christmas tree.
The lamentations of my fourth book were a melting of walls.
Back home, where it's soft.
We've been here all along.

Hey, if we look at the sun at the same time
we'll have a tent (Milenko, Andraž, Marko, David).
That plants don't count is my greatest
reproach to Teilhard de Chardin.
Fish have a heart,
windows have a heart,
night has a heart,
a spike for mountain climbing and a sled have hearts.
A kiss,
dummy.

July 30, Andraž

my brother strides naked
beautiful as a virgin spring
through the hall, kills the lamb
with love

we eat and meditate on the image

sleds rust between winters, the sky gets lower
and grows damp
the earth bears strawberries
soldiers stand hungry
among daffodils yellow as night
a clear, pure guard

shutters, closed and locked
trail markers in the woods and mountains
O Mt. Čaven, air crowded with angels

army tracks, bread, bread
O Sibyil, split hardened color
immovable, unalterable itch

Branko

I see my father climbing onto the wheel of a buzz saw,
he jumps up in his wet knickers and shouts,
"A cupola, Milarepa, cupola, and a green valley,
this is where we'll get moss for our manger."

"The kids are freezing, leave it, Branko, a fog is
rising, it's getting dark and I have dinner to make.
There'll be time for moss, if the weather's good we can
come next week, now get down off there, scoot."

This is where barbed wire encircled Ljubljana, see,
here is where the Germans stood guard. The Germans drink
puddles and while we sleep at night they slither toward us
headfirst. Recently we found two of them in the linen closet,

the third escaped, he stole a compass and the stairs
sagged beneath him, he had to climb our garden fence.
When he got back he threw himself down
pale and winded on his steel cot and said:

"What a marvelous library, what valuable books,
what greasy snails." Germans have a ramified mind, power
plants, they stab Slavs with static electricity till the
tsar says: "Pogrom! Cut the Germans' ears off and slaughter them."

In Central Europe

When you cross through the grass in Central Europe, you see
mountains, forest cabins, the breaking of light.
On long rainy days deer eat from your hand
alongside macadam roads.

Priests, firewood, carnations,
emigrants climb on board,
children with heavy backpacks toss apple
cores out train windows.

In Central Europe the people are secured with wires,
August is always past,
you still feel resentful toward the dancers, Lake
Vrba, Bled.

You're like a plate Bolinas, venomously green Sacramento,
full of oil, Yosemite, stifling steam,
when the bamboo grows,
when the bamboo reaches the sipapuni
when each rings reaches the sipapuni
the door.

[untitled]

My boundary stones are the sun.

The king arrives in a golden coach
and falls into a pond where cattle perish.

[untitled]

Every wild man who singes his heart is worth two glasses of beer

Sheep are too narrow to be roasted evenly

King of Birds

Decadence is haziness. What do you babble
and pile on bricks for, as if they were
entrails of differentiated strata which
almost wrung you out, caught you in a sticky,

meager trap, sucked you up, you dumb-ass insect.
You have paid 51 cents for milk which is
good, much better than the last time when
you paid 54 cents. First cut off this tree.

With total devotion read a list and an
itemized bill of things which belong
to Cornelius Doremus, baptized in
Acquackonock in 1774. You won't be

knocked down, a color will carry you
arund the world immediately. There will
be no diagrams trickling slowly like
pitch from a cork tree, and if there

are, they'll be there at once. There is
no need to fertilize the image. The image
doesn't need rain. It's got to be created
out of nothing. It has to be stamped

like a seal of the universe. Like this
dance of the king of birds. He didn't
waddle on earth, he didn't get dust on
his feet with history. We get him directly

from Lesbos. On the way he only visited
his friend, Catullus. He is the highest
leap in this magic sphere, named Iowa City,
he is the most glittering Bob Perelman.

Poem

All those fabulous *cordons sanitaires* of civilization,
such as Yugoslavia, Java, the court at Bucharest, are
destined for vermin. The jungle reaching for us
knows taller trees than our pines. Hummingbirds

more colorful than eagles will peck at our
wounds. Names like zebrine whiteness, Guaporé,
Punta Arenas, will entwine the Freising monuments
and choke the ivy on them. Disinterred

Partisans will have their rumps smashed, for
want of genitals. Love will give way to sparks,
drums to jungle. The yellow race to the white race,

black race to yellow. And for you who will be
summoning this poem, lost at the crossroads, facing paths
that promise only guts, brains to fire.

1971

[untitled]

Great poets
foretell their own deaths in a single line.
When they wear down,
exhaust their guardian angel so it sleeps,
they pierce through the earth with truth.

No hand stretches out and shoves
the signs back into the dark, loved ones sleep
covered by their dreams as though in mossy valleys.

They don't hear the lightning,
don't start,
don't shudder at the breakthrough
when the seal strikes.

Maruška bewitches and disassembles me before I see.
In service to love and fear
she stands fierce as a hunter of doormice,
and with a blow from her club she stops me at the edge.

Yucatan

Maruška, Ana, Francie, Bob and me
we're going to Mexico for Christmas '71
I'll meditate on people I like, watch
the desert through a pane of glass, Ana will piss

I'll meditate on sin crushed in a white glow
for I love Bob, I'll love the moon's body when she's
as grown up as Maruška, we're rested
tired of lifting the dam between soul and meat

tender, as though blessed with wine
grateful, a clean mellow fruit in the new
balance between earth and sky, hiding before
hostile waiters of gasoline, wounded by the

glitter of freedom of our bodies, persisting
in hostile jealousy, we're traveling, cradling
laughing, with a river of tigers swinging
sliding south, living birth

[untitled]

Who's better,
a god with a beard or a god without a beard?
A god with a beard.

Christmas Poem

toad, honey, bread, salt
a clock rings

he falls swings and wavers
on the branch
curled up and dirty

he touches the penis belonging to his son
and announces the birth
the date when he embarked
into the orbit of love and hate

the day when light and dark
are matter
the breathing-in of moisture
and the beginning of silver
when the Norns sign the check

they deposit colors
making birds float
in fear of direction
and comets glow
thus the miracle breaks loose from the lineage

the orders are definite
the boat is safe

History

Tomaž Šalamun is a monster.
Tomaž Šalamun is a sphere rushing through the air
He lies down in twilight, he swims in twilight.
People and I, we both look at him amazed,
we wish him well, maybe he is a comet.
Maybe he is punishment from the gods,
the boundary stone of the world.
Maybe he is such a speck in the universe
that he will give energy to the planet
when oil, steel, and food run short.
He might only be a hump, his head
should be taken off like a spider's.
But then something would then suck up
Tomaž Šalamun, possibly the head.
Possibly he should be pressed between
glass, his photo should be taken.
He should be put in formaldehyde, so children
would look at him as they do at fetuses,
protei, and mermaids.
Next year, he'll probably be in Hawaii
or in Ljubljana. Doorkeepers will scalp
tickets. People walk barefoot
to the university there. The waves can be
a hundred feet high. The city is fantastic,
shot through with people on the make,
the wind is mild.
But in Ljubljana people say: look!
This is Tomaž Šalamun, he went to the store
with his wife Maruška to buy some milk.
He will drink it and this is history.

Grass

I want to be so pleasant that I become a god
and am lost and forgotten, too.
I write poems because I am a cactus.
People are moist for each other
that's why they kiss each other on the lips.
I don't even know how to fix coffee for myself,
and it's hard to live with me.
Maruška suffers, Ana doesn't.
As if a tiger were throwing the discus and
playing with it lazily, determining its altitude.
But a tiger has no hands and doesn't know how to,
can't do that, a tiger has a heart and teeth.
Rivers flow through me and fructify me
and everything is green, green grass.
When I am sad, I get up
and wander through the world.
I am not ready for death at all,
but I can take that draught at any time,
like soup the nanny gives me.
Death must smell like a waterfall.
Death must smell like mother.
Nothing bitter pursues me.
Now I am four years old.
Four and a half,
the son of the man I love.
If I were any older, he would have to be
over twenty-two years old.
But I want him to stay forever young
and handsome and stern as he is today,
so I'll always be only this old.
I am a Russian, because he is.
Cindy brought me coffee, because I am
concentrating so hard that I am radiating through the whole house,

into the yard, onto the park and the squirrels that
Ana is going to play with when Maruška comes by boat.
We'll live together and I shall say:
Ain't no mamba snake in America.

September 20, 1972

Anselm Hollo, Josephine Clare, Custer the dog and Rudie
the cat helped me get born yesterday, to
be saved, I hope. They hugged me and talked
and talked with me. Learning and rowing, lying in
the lap of god, looking around, sniffing, loving
and twitching my ears like a rabbit. This is my life,
such enormous pleasure that I'd die at once if I strayed.
Poets fall in love with poets and get badly
hurt. One poet reincarnates the other. Reincarnation
is when love, a pure white light, hurls you back
to the womb and turns you inside out like a glove. The light sucks
you into death and then expels you. In Iowa City yesterday,
September 20, 1972, I, Tomaž Šalamun, underwent a sacramental
                    murder and
resurrection. Oh lordy, hallelujah, I've been born again, I'm soft
and vulnerable. This miracle was all spring in coming.
In America, in England, in Yugoslavia, with love's
mad energy, with horrible pains. This is the second
miracle that Peter Trias has found the energy to adjure.
The first occurred in Greece to Peter's schoolmate Aleksej
and that is documented. He barely missed being ruined.
Most of my writing in the last three weeks was
dictated and when I was writing my epitaph, I looked at
the finished product, and suddenly understood. I was seized
by a terrible, savage panic. I wrote Peter a letter
in which I told him that murder was a sacrament, no one's fault,
that I loved him, and I got in the car and drove off. The panic
was so awful I felt as though I was being blown
apart, my legs were burning, and something was about to explode in
my chest. A minute before it did I drove off
onto the grass. The earth began to quake, I sensed
Anselm like a morning star and
like an awestruck sacred cow set off on foot to meet him. We talked

of fate and summoned grace. They gave me vodka
and gin to drink and when I awoke I was wet
as though with dew, like a pure child in a silver mountain forest.
Anselm put Joan Baez on the record player.
I thought of Maruška and Ana, and Josephine and Anselm,
of Peter and Joan and I was grateful. I hope I'll be
good, that our life will be pleasant, that we'll be attentive
to each other, and kind. I thought of my mother and
father, my brother and sister, and Grandma. And Elliot
and Cindy. How much one has to suffer, how irresponsible
and conceited I was. How many people close to me
I injured. The earth shakes, the earth shakes with a miracle!
The holy dread goes on.

[untitled]

My mind skis from village to village,
eats cashews, defines leaves,
my mind runs from continent to continent
and makes little wicker baskets out of snow.
Maruška,
wounded Ophelia,
memory calls us.

[untitled]

My mind is a woman, a male Medici,
trained to be an archer, a faun,
it has five eyes:
two of a polecat,
two of a crow,
and the first, the terrible one of the Cyclops.

[untitled]

My mind has the scent of an altar triptych.
Woodcutters plant
wooden sticks in leather.
On wooden sticks
they hang iron rings,
on iron rings
they tie
green horses.

My mind is power dripping with boiling kasha.
My guardian angel, dear,
let him rest,
good spirit,
let him rest.

[untitled]

My mind has the scent of a white flower,
it fixes green blood on black stalks,
to the black blood it invites hungry hogs,
red horses.

My mind is a sacred cow,
bleeding in the ellipsis.

[untitled]

All these are gifts.
I am high in the mountains.
Woods, washed over with
white rush like a banjo.
I came home and thought:
my sister has been lobotomized,
my brother has been lobotomized,
my whole family has been lobotomized.
But they had not been lobotomized,
only their feather had fallen out.
Images devour classifications
like cannibals, devour horsemen who pass
like cannibals.
There are no brakes left.
My eyes draw the soul like a pail of water.
I mix it with bricks.
No mortar juts out of it,
no body hair looks out at its ankles.

The Rabbit

Snakes have polyvinyl shoulders on their backs
and carry green unripe apricots in them.
They write letters to the bank in Florence day and night.
Rabbits are crossing the Nile by the billions
and perishing, so that one rabbit gets across.
One of them sniffs and says, "I'm sniffing."
One of them drinks and says, "I'm drinking."
One of them jumps on a drum like a sacred cow
and says, "Where are my antlers?
Should I even have them as a rabbit?"
And a mother rabbit throws a rosemary
bud at his head and who can tell
if it was done in anger or from love?
It comes across as this:
get down off that drum, you rabbit, and we'll pet you.
But the rabbit is so far away.
The rabbit eats his paws dipped in ketchup
and dances like a tiger.
He has a "bandage" (Fr.) over his eyes, and
pins in his ears and worms and moles, and stars
tied to moles' legs with string go jingling.
And he jumps at the membrane and falls back, thump!
And he goes to heaven and says, "It's not warm enough here,"
and he jumps out, thump! And he develops stigmata and
he squirts through them like a water pistol,
so that all the books get wet and warped
and soaked and they surrender unconditionally.
The rabbit gives birth to ether and has terrible labor pains,
so bad they set the library at Alexandria
on fire. Lesser people tighten their asses
and say, "Damned stupid rabbit."

Young Men

O people, the sky
certainly does not slide, or crunch.
In winter, the snow crunches,
the sky only trembles. Splashes. Birds
are like velvet, fixed on velvet.
Vallejo developed a theory on how to
skip out of the Metro so that the sidewalk
would not destroy his heels.
Did he drive his limbs farther than rails?
Would the sky unreel, like a cord
if we could reel it, like a cord
around metaphors, and little lambs?
All right, let us say the sky will never
get busy. But are men, therefore,
louder or more silent?
Is this worker, building a road, being led?
And who are whale, dog, cat? The glue
for the young of whale, dog, cat?
Saint Augustine's skeleton? Only colors
of a patch? Young men beckon
an awful lot. Then they grow old
and die, and if they really stare at
the beckoning of the living
finally it only steals our time.
In any case, this table would fall apart
if the eyes of the curious were caught in it
like chisels. Time would cease round
and we would bump into it
turned over, like Amen.

[untitled]

A tribe, an insufficient velvet, borders
on a plain loaded with gas. Astonishment
strains like a bow. Trembling crumbles
the descriptive geometry of the sacred city.

You who are clarity, you stand before
the wall. You who are offered grass
for the anointed barbarous dogs, you are the norm
in the scorching heat. Unstitch the epicenter,

set sail, azure! Drink mountain glaciers, home!
A territory, the instrumentalized grace is power
of feedback, and to have not is only the first
temptation of the too easily extravagant. Attention!

The city will have risen on the slope. The light,
tender with gravitation, will not swallow the tribe
glued up on the edge, with stoical haughtiness.
The water is a guillotine. I am the food of great masses.

About the Slavs

A rubber kitten, meooow!
Elephants are turning on a merry-go-round,
their feet hand toward the center.
To gobble down some kind of weight
and to assault history?
Does it make this dame happier,
less blue?
The history of Slavs is, for example,
utterly miserable.
Miserable and dark,
sad.
Some small nations biting
each other, because the weather is bad.
Hustling and bustling, grouchy.
The gruffness is their history,
the result of bad upbringing, of course!
So, Slavs, out of history!
Back to life under the tent, back to nature!
Eat bison steaks, so your teeth will again
be white and shining,
so that your heart can again,
at full speed: boom, boom!

Air

Your body is the duct in which
wheat, naptha, and food flows,
the bridge over which the horseman races.
Your hands are the window,
your words are the window,
your body is the window.
Whatever you touch or caress in your mind
burns in a terrible flame and smells.
In every breath,
in every gesture you guide me.
And you bend,
and I bend,
and I get up,
and I get up and go.
You tell me not to use inflated, hungry language,
dry weapon of the air.
You tell me to be careful.
You tell me to be kind and I am kind.
You tell me to be wealthy and I am wealthy.
Blue and powerful are my fortresses,
I slip through the souls of kings,
I travel from Babylon to Nineveh,
from Nineveh to Babylon.
You appointed me:
I am handsome and haughty,
because I am strong and wet.
Your body is a duct in which
wheat, naptha, and food flows,
a bridge over which the horseman races.
Your hands are the window,
your words are the window,
your body is the window.
Whatever you touch or caress in your mind
burns in a terrible flame and smells.

Charles d'Orléans

Charles d'Orléans goes into the rock
and barricades himself. Emotions are
cyclic, and on levels. Deer are shot
with bows and die. A drop on the tongue ·

and evaporation from the drop into
the tongue makes the Rocky Mountains.
History and sight are colors, genitals
in the brain. Even if I take off

a genre or sadness, a rhythm or color,
material sizzles in the pan, it is
a kiss of eyes. Socrates falls down,

is tripped. Therefore: *Nonchaloir,* not blood.
And turquoise of course, not the legality
of barbarians. Listen: Scythians are edible.

Imperialism Takes Off My Head

In the morning, when I awake,
I feel the monster has been translated.
He melted, decomposed, and translated himself.
I cannot call him back,
he lies on the other side, lazy pig,
I cannot call him back.
You do not eat the grass anymore.
The meadow is burned by the welding machine.
You do not eat my mouth and sound,
you do not lick my ears, little girl.
You cannot break through, into the sun,
but you feed on some interplanetary
contingent of swamp shells.
Light the fires,
beautiful people of the world,
light the fires.
Warm the fields against frost,
pray that the Slovenian tongue will not expire.
Touch me with your hand, Maruška,
be tender with me, good spirit.
I bewitched you in the open,
made love to you with a god's head,
but you got scared, my bride, my tongue.
I made you a king, gave you ships and battles,
built you a road back to the Hittites,
but you were afraid the elephant would trample you.
Contorted dry monkey, deserter, technician,
a narrow background frustrated you.
Lingua franca gives me air,
lingua franca gives me shelter,
lingua franca anoints me with oil.
Lingua franca strikes the soul of men with lightning.
I step in and eat,

I step in and eat and bewitch and enjoy.
Lingua franca takes my head off, takes me out of this hole
where fat collects.
Where the sparks cannot get through.
Be beautiful, be courageous, my language.
Embrace me, hold me,
be my skin,
beam energy without these chains.

Kraków

Gombrowicz, proszę, Pana, jest chorym
czlowiekiem, out of his mind. It is
his fault Poland looks the way it does
today. I read him in Edinburgh, where

my late husband taught anatomy.
We couldn't have turned our parks
into Victory Gardens regardless of
the outcome of the war. Thomas Mann

was more depressed every day. He never
revealed himself in the letters to Mme.
Flukowska as much as he did to me.
My daughter made a decision and went

to fight in Yugoslavia. When she lost
her first husband, she married
a second. I was not able to replace
my Jacusz, even in my dreams. So we have

Communists in the family. And if I got it
right, my granddaughter Heda this summer
almost married an Indian who had come
flying to London on BOAC

stark naked. Better translate
Norwid. He means so much to your
Mom. I lived with Jews, too, studying
under Bourdelle, but I knew not to go
too far. They didn't know how not to go too far.

Cold

Land, snake, river,
sweeten the loam.
The sickle breaks,
the wheat bursts.
Ships are dark with silver.

A whoosh of owls, a rainbow made of wolves
inspires Magna Carta.
The totem slavers on the werewolf's head.
Turn the barrel around,
milky alpha.

Pubs are for us,
cold is for winter.
Summer is for geese.
They sway, they coo,
they put Scotch tape where it burns.

Sand

I am not the subject.
I am God's strongbox.
Like a cow, I have to lie
on gold, at the precise
altitude. It isn't true
that I am here on the sand
because I would love it.
I am the pumpkin
on the hot roof of the world.
The Lord drips water on me.
I am not the subject.
I am God's strongbox.
I made no decision to look
either down or up.

[untitled]

You're taking the piece of iron, right?
It's red. So, it was red before too, right?
And what is red? Red is only a part of white, right?
Iron is a bit of snow. You are a bit of white.

Snow

I melted the snow!
I melted the snow!
I melted the white, white snow!
Rum.

Silent, invisible rum,
the tempest.
A window.
Obelisk-rum.

I melted the snow!
I melted the white snow!
You, you,
timid sky blue hands,
the rum of reason.

You, birds!
Timid, sky blue roses!

Nikola Tesla

When St. Francis took off his coat,
he wasn't cold. His previous life was cold
boiling to turn into wine.
When it turned into wine, moles came to drink,
grasshoppers, cats, too, who in the Middle Ages
were led around on a chain
because they used to be lions.
People were afraid cats would eat them.
Not true, cats never ate people.
Only those lazy little monks copied the texts
so inattentively that a lot of rust appeared,
just like on great ocean liners.
Truly, cats were lions, silky ones.
There were small sewing baskets beside them
even when they were grazing in the desert.
They grazed in that they licked the sand
like hens when they need calcium.
The hens lie on their sides in the dark.
The lights are on in all the houses.
Nikola Tesla, through hard work, scratched out
electricity just like people who shell peas
separating the pea from the pod.
All done, he said. This is electricity! Amen.
Now turn off the lights and go to sleep.

The Word

The Word is the one and only foundation of the world.
I am its servant and its master.
And though the spirit sends out atoms
to smell, touch and feel, we are

equal to gods in this field.
Language is not encountering anything
new. There is no final judgment,
no superior. The assumption

is in the concentric, in everything
we see, and we don't see more than
a grain of sand. Things in their gazing seem closer,
but that is not the criterion. I repeat: things

are not the criterion. The criterion is
inside us, as the ultimate dispersion.
Death was named mistakenly by those
to whom the light was hidden.

Oops!

Poets, marry sorceresses, either that or be
homosexual. I've given it a lot of thought, there
is no other way. Maruška is a sorceress. Which is to say
she vanishes in unknown waters or breaks out

like a fire, bright—in short, she always finds a way out.
At times she complains that a fearful weariness of Šalamun
has seized her, that her eyelids hurt when she moves them,
and I, perplexed and shamefaced, have to think what it is

I do, and how badly it might have turned out if I hadn't found
my sorceress. Only amateurs believe the amount of
writing holds pace with the rate of murder. No,
corpses decay, making poets sad, ineffectual,

they take to drink, and drunken poets are like drunken
tailors. They merely waste material.
Homosexuality has one advantage: souls commune
without upsetting nature, which can be nice, but altogether

risky, very risky, and really close to shit. Far better
than a fat-assed maiden sitting on your belly
and crushing you, but as I've said:
it carries the same element of risk as marrying a sorceress.

Epistle to the Angry Ones

My brain is a butterfly, a soft precious material
a transparent silk. Swinging your clubs can
really damage it, or at least destroy my day.
Can you imagine a butterfly, which gets worn out

by the strategy of armored units holding back
a beast as furious as Professor Ziherl, whom I love
in principle. Every lost pulsation is a sin, every
lost chance to rest on a blossom is a classic example

of social pathology. My brain is the universe, wider
than blue. It kindly watches the white sharks tiring
themselves out in the seaweed because the Lord gave every
tiny animal the right to eat. It's miles and miles

between the seaweed and the phoenix. The white shark
is not even a dolphin which could snare ordinary flying
fish in its lovely arc. This man will die sad and
hungry if he chooses from such an impossible menu.

Turbines

The planet repenting is the planet cracking.
A mouth, turbines are left over. Honey drips,
and when I discovered the iron rings were
for horses, I took a purple coffin and stuck

pronouns together. It might be useful to us
like a fern is useful to us. For fleas, for
a sceptre, for Jesus Christ. Father and son,
chopped, father and son, wrapped up in the

same bag. Jesus Christ made it. Peter crumpled
his penis and remained a director. The plains
which are present, a descriptive geometry, swallowed
by fatigue. The earth is nervous, but the mind is spinal.

Car le vice

Car le vice, rongeant ma native noblesse,
is at fault for this snarling, this flapping of wings.
All day long I boast and whoop and dance,
at sunset I stop short: a white square of white blueness

harpooned like a whale. A tiny pin no bigger
than a diamond makes a histological specimen
of my soul. Hey! How do you even survive then,
my dearest, how do you regenerate?

Such are the incredibly pathetic questions
Tomaž Šalamun puts to his soul to get
to the bottom of things. But there is no thing. Or

bottom. Only this edifying fable of the creative process,
with which sooner or later every immortal can destroy
his onlookers. In order to soar in peace, *il Terribile.*

Birthdays

For my twenty-fifth birthday in the Army
I got: a mirror with a specially nice frame,
encrusted with seashells, deer, and a brook;
furlough, a *kremschnitte,* a glass of wine.
I watched the movie about Jean Harlow who died
a victim of excessive bleaching of her hair.
Men who give much to mankind are tired,
lonely at the end. Sometimes all bleach comes
back, and kills them.
Four years later on my birthday I thought:
New York City is a lot like the Yugoslav National Army.
A lot of people you never met before.
Rauschenberg showed us Twombly's paintings
of the early Fifties. Everybody has gone
to Long Island. It was hot.
Tatyana Grosman showed us the street
from the terrace where she lived two years
after the war without documents. Nobody
believed that she was Tatyana Grosman.
If anybody had killed her, it wouldn't
have been possible to prove that he had killed
anybody. Then I came back to Thirty-Fourth Street, lay down,
smoked, and listened to *Tommy,* The Who.
Maybe I'm writing this because it's so rainy.

The North

The North which looks toward the North
is strict and blunt as a photo flash.
Apparently sharp, mute, and swift as lightning,
aggressive and white, apparently full of magnesium,

a waterfall in the vacuum, I say.
It weaves, it weaves, I give. In the middle
of the process my mind runs away to cigarettes
which I forgot, breaks the membrane and hurts

concentration: it itself starts from my back,
it itself starts from my shoulders, it
itself jumps and strikes, as only an imperfect
body does, which at first rouses more

interest than the real one, because of noise,
because of white foam striking,
and here is the North, strict and blunt.
It sticks on white foam which it recognizes,

because it can make an imprint in it.
Peace is every chunk of iron
where the trains rush. Which is
the North which looks toward the North, strict and blunt.

Bitches Angels

Angels' entrails hung out like linen
will never be white. In winter they freeze
and don't drip, but this is their greatest
extent of hygiene. In accordance

with the first proposition, angels come back
and peck at them. In accordance with the second,
they sell them to ants, for their brains,
in big auctions. Those propositions are there

because of sin, a tattooed stupidity,
which came from a censored reading of sacred texts.
I don't account for my slaughter,

you don't account for your slaughter.
Why, then, should angels return?
To walk beside you?

[untitled]

White,
older brother of a wedding guest,
don't wait for mist,
don't wait for rice.

Painted Desert

When we got to the Painted Desert
I remembered Heidegger.
And I said to Maruška: I want to run
naked in the sun through the desert
and I remembered Antonioni's frightened
movie, but I still relished the idea
of being naked in the sand.
And Maruška said: don't do that,
you asshole. Do you think I'll watch
you disappear over the horizon
and chase you in the sand?
And I said, both of us will go.
And what about Ana?
We'll leave her in the car and give
her cookie. Cookie was
Ana's drink.
And I said, it's really dangerous
but your maternal instincts are strong
enough and you will immediately run
back to Ana.
If I feel weak just chase me over the sand.
I remembered Heidegger and Ed Dorn.
Ouch! How hot was the sun, how dizzy.
The desert is a fantastic orgasm!
Ana really laughed. The sky was almost black.
The air was black.
The Painted Desert is pink. Its name
is the Painted Desert, but if you stay
in the sand, the sand is not pink
but demonic. If you stretch out
in the sand, the sand is demonic.
I remember how once, when I still
lived in those huge rooms, I pretended

to be Gregor Samsa with such temperance
that Braco became really pale. And I
asked him for some salad, and both of us
went down to the street because Braco
thought I would sober up but I went on
and stopped a passer-by, and I told him
I was Gregor Samsa. Braco became a total
ash pastel, he was sure I'd flipped out,
and that's true. If he hadn't knocked me
down in front of the Nun's Church
and made me dizzy and enraged, but I was
grateful too, who knows if I would
have come down. And Braco vomited and
I saw he really loved me and I was sorry
and scared. I didn't know things had
gone so far. I jumped back into the car.
Maruška was like a bronze and Ana howled.
Maruška was totally self-controlled,
hardly trembling. She calmly drove the car
like a hearse thirty miles south on Route 66,
and stopped at the gas station. And with
her hands still on the steering wheel she said:
put your clothes on. And I knew she was
not a witch, she loved me. Sometimes this
exhibitionism will sweep me away like
the wind brushes away a ball of cotton.
And then we spent five days in the Grand
Canyon all calm and tender, and I was
taking pictures of Maruška all the time,
and so the most beautiful pictures
of America are those where Maruška stands
on the edge of the Grand Canyon in that beige
crocheted dress, which we bought on Stari
Trg, Ljubljana, and I also bought her
a Hopi bracelet and a Hopi ring,
and Ana a lot of ice cream.

To Tender Bambi's Eyes, to the White Father

There is never a desert around
the real Pope, only frisky cardinals
devouring chicken. The oasis is
certainly not a horn. People live

in trees or in a box; however, the Pope
changes his position with the elevator.
Cola di Rienzo was nuts. Savonarola
was much stronger, but a child.

Nobody is as huge as the Pope who
incessantly pushes the buttons of the
elevator. The Pope offers himself up
as good-hearted to the faithful.

Intelligent men spit him out like pear
seeds, shaking their democratic heads.
But the Pope is really like a Boeing.
His white cap is hydraulic.

1/1/73

Good morning sun!
Good morning, New Year!
Good morning, all friends on earth,
all enemies, and the meager, good morning!
Good morning, Maruška, when you wake up,
good morning, Ana, kitten!
Hi, Ron!
Good morning, all Slovenians on the earth!
Good morning, Bob!
Good morning, Francie!
Good morning, Anselm & Josephine!
We are: boom in the New Year!
Good morning, squirrels!
Good morning, Mom & Father,
Good morning, Grandma!
Good morning, Stane Dolanc,
I wish you would bring some gentleness
to Yugoslavia.
Good morning to you again,
because you oppress the people,
you must stop oppressing the people!
Good morning, Ljubljana!
Don't despair, good morning!
Good morning, Čoban, don't be sad.
Good morning, dear young Slovenian poets,
don't allow yourselves to get frustrated!
Good morning, all ecclesiastically minded ones,
all you, Party members,
good morning from the bottom of my heart!

Raw Sienna

When we grow up, we'll bomb Paris,
rockets will open the cellar door.
We'll paint the roof white,
we'll paint the water's gullet black.

When we grow up, we'll bomb Paris,
roasted doves will rest on the terrace.
We'll tie a huge paper ribbon on a sleigh,
a beam of oblique sunlight will spread in the samovar.

[untitled]

Little robin,
bones pinned to the cosmos.
Who whistles, who calls?

[untitled]

I am an innocent little girl,
the fiancée of Tomaž Šalamun.
As long as I behave myself,
he'll be as strong as Cheops.

Maria

I

This is a book
for little girls.
The most beautiful
and
perversely soft
book
for their eyes only.
Block-chested
deer
sprout from the earth.
They drop their load
and leave the mess,
but I can't tell
if they were here
or not.

II

I'm a
bilberry.
I'm the black
sweet berry
under the pine
in the forest.
I still have time,
two days in fact,
before the little girl
or the shepherd
passes with a cup
and a comb.

III

I'm the she-mouse
who by a long
tunnel fell
on the soft grass.
With my little
teeth I licked
the stovepipe.
With my little claws
I scratched the
wall on a day
of roses.

IV

I stood on the
bottom of the fence
and watched
the cold blue peacock butterfly
up above.
Clouds rushed
behind his wings.
I lay down
head against the fence.
I drank all
the mother's milk,
all the earth's oil.

V

And in the snare
that juts out of the corner
of the stovepipe,
I saw the mousetrap.
Out of a hole in heaven,

rain fell.
I hit it
with a straw
so it turned rusty,
standing open
on the rowen
like old grass
which the cattle
forgot to graze.

VI

I placed
on the anvil
a lady's slipper.
I hit it so
hard sparks
flew when I
drove the hobnails.
How come
there's a light
in the dark stovepipe
under the earth.
I didn't think
there'd be
a slipper
in my fate.

VII

Then I gave
birth to a little one
through my rectum
and put him on the
dark bottom
of the pipe.

I hewed a playpen
for him on
the shiny grass.
I stuck flags
in the humus
next to each
wooden leg.
I rested
hand on my hip.
With hand on my
hip I looked
up.

VIII

Most likely
the flying birds
were black
freckles.
I ripped the pacifier
out of my son's mouth
which ruined the position
of my hand on my hip.
He rocked himself
with a pacifier in his hand
the span of five fingers.

IX

How is it
possible
to sleep
on soft grass
in the sunless
black earth?
Can one see

the light
of the other heaven?
I'm the red
she-mouse.
I have more pink
than any other animal.
With pink paws,
pink whiskers,
I'm not even a mole.

X

Surround me
tightly
my snow-laden
blue-shattered
leaves.
I'm the
dark-red
unprotected
wild strawberry.
Who will fondle me,
who will touch me
and who will yet
pick me
is not certain.

The Color of Time

From here the apple of
the world will pop out and roll over
generations.
You as well as I
stuffed bags in our eyes.
We cut down pine trees.
We scraped the rust from mouse traps.
We cut the black plasma's teeth out.
Twice I attacked
a thick clod with my scythe
to split it open.
I was rolling lambs and calves over
messengers, who were deeply touched.
They surrendered. And their painted mouths,
bitter wine, ran over. Then I flung
a spear to the robust moon so I'd know
the exact time.
That's how I know.
Time is tall and yellow, the child
of the sun, the sun itself.

My First Time in New York City

My first time in New York City
I was scared shitless.
I took the bus to the terminal,
changed and took another bus to the YMCA.
Luckily there was a TV camera in the elevator so I didn't get mugged.
My first time in New York City, when I took
the bus to the terminal,
then the bus from there to the Y,
and finally the elevator with the TV camera in the Y so I wouldn't get
        mugged,
I went to my room,
then straight to the shower.
I was showering in the shower and a black man
walked by, smacking and licking his lips.
And I went outside
and steam was hissing out through the vents in the asphalt
and yellow taxicabs were
speeding past,
so that I barely made it across the street
and entered the store
with a sign out front
BOOKS,
where I wanted to buy an album on Fra Angelico,
I remember the
eleven
and twelve-year-old kids
standing in front of the
store
laughing so hard that they
kept slapping their thighs.
My first time in New York City
I gave out all my cigarettes within half an hour.
And I finally

managed to sniff out
where the poetry store was.
And I went into the poetry store and
as casually
as I could, I said
Hi!
and two bizarrre little men
stared out at me
from where they stood, surrounded by dusty books
and they asked me if I was scared shitless.
No, I said
and I was scared shitless
and I showed them a long letter from Ferlinghetti
and I asked
if they knew anyone
who could translate me into English from Slovene.
And I was scared shitless
and they said wait
and they asked me how to say butterfly
in Slovene
and I told them the Slovene
for elk,
because I knew
that half an hour from now they might meet
some Yugoslav
diplomat on the street
and tell him
that they know
the Slovene word for
butterfly
and I would be burned then at the stake back home as a witch.
That people
returning from my funeral
wouldn't even be able to make it home
because before they could
they would all have strokes from grief.

And in fact, before long
Ralph Donofrio,
a tall,
handsome
man
resplendent in a huge rust-colored hat
walked into the Phoenix on Jones Street.
Right away the mannikins handed him
the letter from Ferlinghetti
to read.
I asked him quickly if he knew Slovene
and he said
listen man,
come with me
so we can talk in private.
And I went with him to Hick Street
in Brooklyn Heights
and we pored over Fitch's translations and we
translated the rest
and once during all this I went to Central Park
and another time, deep in thought, I walked across
the Brooklyn Bridge
and both times something went
click! click!
and I
suddenly
saw
with perfect
clarity
that it was only a matter of time before
New York City would vomit me forth
into the sky
like a star.

The Level Road

I drank blood.
I drove a truck.
The stars snowed down on me.
Some day the water will be extinguished,
and all that's left will be the gaps.
The upper part of the arch,
half a ring,
dry air minus memory.
It will all be clear and precise
as in Sappho.
One's heart will beat
in tasteless color photographs.

Astrophysics and Us

What astrophysics conceives of
as its background,
its canvas,
was my cradle.
It's true, at first I didn't grow,
I only kept expanding.
They stuffed slippers in my mouth
because of a computing error.
Because of Pythagoras's students' promiscuity.
I've documented that,
capped it
and set it 2,500 years down.
My laurel wreathes have had no problems
in all that time, in fact.
Gold on greenery eases breathing.
Here you have the focus of panic,
of alchemy as a condemnatory papal bull
which the dislocation of the Renaissance defined as a foil,
a world bank.
I, not you, Ezra Pound,
have lived to see the time of the commingling of all things.

Luiza

I was sitting on the potty, although I
must have been five years old by then.
Luiza, an old friend of Father's, stopped by
our court. Father gave her the cold shoulder
and told her right away
she'd grown old.
Luiza shuddered and took my mother
by the hand, so that
a smooth, shiny, perhaps leaden
pyramid took shape connecting the pot,
mother and Luiza,
and then began to rotate quickly on its axis.
I blushed, stood up from the pot
and ran to our maid for comfort.
Apparently my parents and Luiza
soon forgot about their quarrel (and me, as well),
and made plans for an outing, the three of them.
And in fact, the next morning after breakfast
they set out to climb a tall mountain.
Father tied together mother's and Luiza's
hands with willow branches
and the pyramid began to hiss
and melt away.
Father had a radio along and asked on it
if anything was up.
A page deliberately described to him,
as though dictating word for word, how
the pyramid was melting. Father ordered him
to stop the very moment it disappeared.
And then all three came back home, ruddy-faced,
happy, tousled by the mountain wind.

[untitled]

I implore the masters
of this world to be gentle.
Why should I

have to live in a world
that despises
the life of the spirit?

Why have I
been able to write only
20 percent of my poems

at home
and been forced
forever to flee

the land
I would just as soon
love

most of all,
or suffocate?
Why do I sense

that irrational
fear,
resistance

to freedom and
human worth?
This poem is a special

petition

and grievance.
It derives from the shock

and dread
I experience
over and over

whenever I lick the wounds
from traumas back home.
Many of us

feel this way.
Accept this petition
and grievance

from all of us
Gastarbeiter.

November 11, 1954

November 11, 1954, at ten p.m.:
I was coming home from the Partisan gym.
I was wearing a tweed sport coat,
and under the tweed sport coat
a violet-blue sweatshirt.
A man stopped me
between Loggia and the movie house,
he seemed a little drunk.
He said he'd come from Genoa.
Suddenly he was all over me,
put his hand over my mouth
and dragged me to the entryway
of what's now the Civic Library.
To start with, he ate my sweater.
The wool was instantly
transformed into snow flakes, which fluttered
in the air as they fell to the pavement.
They produced a crystalline sound,
they seemed to be made of wood, not snow,
farther back in the entryway they seemed to be cut out of poster
        board.
When they had formed a ground cover
about a foot deep,
he clapped his hands.
The mass of them hardened into a mirror.
At the mirror's center a rectangular
gilt frame appeared —
it was very bright —
and a star began to rotate.
As its ultra-high shriek
pierced my whole being,
a self-portrait of the
eighteen-year-old Dürer appeared.

Dürer was alive,
he wiggled his fingers, which were not in
the portrait itself,
but in an isolated expanse of mirror
connected to the rest.
I started to shake from cold,
and in the meantime the man from Genoa had eaten
my sweater and sport coat.
Suddenly he seemed tired and bored
and slowly began to fade away.

Braco!

How does that dot grow,
that plait,
that fold,
that bone,
that ray,
a new center,
which as you told me
came surging from your work
took root in you and grew like a discovery?
Though I couldn't quite grasp the details,
it was clear you were speaking
of that minute shift,
that infinitely calm
and infinitely terrifying empyreal moment
that shakes the body
because it's there,
birth and spark.

That in a moment transforms water to wine
or a bud into a flower,
so that galaxies clank together with a thud

and man stares speechless,
incredulous
that the flash is so *real*.

I Love You

The record
of heaven's growth
is the movement

of each eyelid
on every
born and unborn

human face.
Not a kitten
or a tree,

or herds
of wild animals
are excluded

or forgotten.
The record
of heaven's growth

is the image
of all pastures,
the image

of all shadows on green
pastures
in heat and darkness.

Every twinge
of each tremor
of the earth,

each cry

of all children destined
for birth.

Don't be sad,
don't worry, Maruška,
savor this moment of grace.

The record
of heaven's growth
is

every drop
of the rainbow
that falls on your brow,

stilling,
separating longing
and love.

[untitled]

Whoever reads me
as ironic
will be guilty

before God.
I am indifferent
to your decadent

defense systems
all that muck
of the parvenu criminal,

which you herald
as humor and the
cornerstore

of your
historical
experience.

The Hymn of Universal Duty

I proclaim the brotherhood of natural, powerful, saintly people.
The glorious union, the union of blinding flashes and holy labor,
the mind and soul of the planet, we, like you, are
a conspiracy of joy,
smaller than a drop of blood.
We (you and I and rain and dust),
we (elk and door and cry and inching snails),
we, who have sloughed off all inert layers,
heal wounded human hearts.
Nor are we hostile to the flame of every age and movement.
We proclaim the world's maturation, its endless growth and stasis,
its silent footsteps in the snow, its thundering falls,
we proclaim the sacred language forever spoken by all people:
I'm afraid, I'm happy, I love you, I want to eat.
Let everything burst forth into the light of day, just as it is,
into the hallowed beauty of a gift of life.
And you, decadent black holes,
minor masters in your knotted sacks,
worn-out captives of niggardly good taste, gambling
for goals,
you we ask out to dance.
As sure as the sun shines in the sky, a child's tear is always pure.
Fear not,
for although your sparks were long since scattered into
a million cubic miles of fear,
our godlike rain will wash you clean.
We bear love and freedom without hate.
And you, blood-leached language,
selling your body from a passion to populate
uncharted lands,
you're wrong!
Dance with us, be our brother,
all colors are united in our hearts.

Acquedotto

I should've been born in Trieste in 1884
on the Acquedotto, but it didn't turn out that way.
I remember the three-storied reddish house,
the ground floor with its furnished living room,
my great-grandfather (my father)
nervously studying the stock market reports,
blowing cigar smoke and calculating quickly.
When I was already four months inside my great-
grandmother, there was a family council,
the result of which was the postponement
of my arrival for two generations.
The decision was written down, the sheet stuffed
into an envelope, sealed and sent to an archive in Vienna.
I remember traveling back toward the light
on my belly, and watching an old man
fussing as he measured the shelf, taking another body from the shelf
and shoving it by the head down the air shaft.
I had the impression I was seven years old,
and that my substitute, my grandfather,
was a bit older, nine or ten.
I was composed. At the same time these events disturbed me.
I remember that for a time I withered,
most likely because of the strong light,
and then my lungs flattened like a bag.
When I reached the proper tonus I fell asleep.
I knew my body was down below,
and in my dream I saw it many times.
It was that of a slow-moving man with mustaches,
a dreamer and banker his whole life.

People

How are you getting here?
People who live in the forest
wear suits. They have
red wings and red caps.
How are you coming?
Are you one of them?
In the forest there are
crowns of thorns for the squirrels,
thickets of blueberry bushes.
They grow. People go
to hell and back.
When they take off their sandals,
nobody knows.

Angel's Method

I tally everything, every death.
I can see you recognize me.
I'm turning gold beneath the eyelids;
my arms hover.
It's my fear that killed you.
The snowslide fell. I'm the sacred cow.
The calves lick me naked.
I no longer have the numerous udders.
Now I've gotten hold of the shroud.
With my elbow through my shirt
I touch your shroud, O sphinx.
A suffering as gentle and as clear as the sky.
Pleasure is a roaring wood stove
that brightens the day.
There's a lady on the pavement,
presumably she wears sandals.
When it comes to joy and generosity, I'm more and more
awkward. I see you with a monstrous
hunk of meat under your shirt.
You're calm and rested like a mask.
Did you roll up your star charts?
Did you take them away?
I poke the air with my finger
to see whether it thickens.
Often I think it will thunder.
I'll end up like a log, or bronze,
being an other.
Continually I'm checking to see
if I still have the canteen on me
so I can take a drink.
You were a soldier once, too.
I was your Unbridled Angel.

[untitled]

Dürer's hare
hisses and falls
from a great height

onto
the linen which will not
sustain it. It

will break
through and explode.
The tent pegs driven in the

earth will
bend. Threads will hang
down toward the green

grass. There is no
wind to muffle the double
shotgun blast

of the hare. The blast of
linen and immediately after it
the blast of its skin

on the earth
or was all that
just to make the threads sway.

I Know

Last night, in the water where Barnett Newman's
line disappeared, I drowned. I swam
to the surface, like a black, dark-blue
luminous blossom. It's terrible to be
a flower. The world stopped.
Mute, like velvet, I opened, perhaps
for good.
Before, with Tomaž Brejc, we
talked about the mystique
of finance, about the eye, the triangle,
about God, possible readings
of chance, of Slovenian history and
destiny.
Don't touch me.
I'm the greatest capital just as I am.
I'm the water in which the
destiny of the world takes place for us.
I'm dizzy. I don't understand.
I know.
Tonight, when I made love, I
reported. I'm a black cube now,
like marble or granite-from-the-other-world,
a bird standing, with yellow
feet and an immense yellow beak, my black
feathers shining; now the eminent church
dignitary, that is:
they all wanted me,
the blossom.
I'm the pure dark blossom
standing still on the surface.
Untouchable and untouched.
Terrifying.

Clumsy Guys

The woman is crying ike a dragon because I'm a poet. No
wonder. Poetry is a sacred machine, the lackey of
an unknown deity who kills as if by conveyer
belt. How many times I'd be
dead, if I hadn't kept cool, taken it easy and
been completely arrogant, so I can with my own instrument
blot my
wings out. Fly, fly ahead, sacred
object, that's not me, I'm reading
The Times and drinking coffee with workers in blue
overalls. They too could easily
kill themselves when they climb a pole to fix
electricity. Sometimes they do. Poets frequently
kill themselves. They scribble on a piece of paper:
I have been killed by too strong a word,
my vocabulary did this to me. So don't tell me these guys
aren't clumsy. You find them in all
professions. Any pedestrian can
kill himself if he doesn't know what
a crosswalk is.

The Stage of the Manichaeans

Poetry, like beauty and
technology, is the field of perfect expression
of all forces in a void. Perfect love requires
no orgasm, the other three do,
they stop at nothing to get it. The cosmos is forever
fascist, because it supports power. A civilization that
loses its territory will perish, unless it
becomes a utopia. U topos, where are we now.
Yet Fourier fabricated
material, and America has caught
China in its lasso. Experiments with drugs
have shown that Hitler was defeated thanks to
the quantity and gradations of the dose, not
suffering. A pyramid is unfathomable.
The triangle and the triangle's eye are
above mankind. Hence revolution is a reasonable
form of management, kept in balance by the cry
of the living. The dead are always premeditated.
Blood alone and the memory of blood can bind them
for a while. All the rest—nirvana or hedonism—
is the fabrication of parallel models which
never meet, however sublime and
useful they may be for longing.
Who can stop technology,
the boundless rice field of divine sustenance.
Revolution is always deliverance, always
memory and the use of memory, and thus
tradition. Poetry draws nourishment from both
fields, though no one knows where it is
defined. In intelligence, which has
veins and cells invested in our brains and
body, just as capital has its interests
invested in Hong Kong, the tundra,

fish, the air itself, or in the self-perpetuating
slashes of the defense mechanism, in screams?
And so: another's blood for my blood—
a sacrifice—and vice-versa: bring me
good gifts—lightning. The difference between
the paleolithic and neolithic periods is
nil. Our civilization is no different
from the Aztec's, nor from that of
the mild and noble berry gatherers.

[untitled]

Emptiness,
my only love,
give me rest.

Folk Song

Every true poet is a monster.
He destroys people and their speech.
His singing elevates a technique that wipes out
the earth so we are not eaten by worms.
The drunk sells his coat.
The thief sells his mother.
Only the poet sells his soul to separate it
from the body that he loves.

The Field of Ptuj

to my great-grandfather, General Franz Von Mally (1821-1893)

You were tired at the very beginning.
When like a trained monkey you posed
with your saber. At the ceremony
when you were made a baron. We forgive you
for looking ridiculous. You thought about duty
and the investment in future generations.
In Zadar you had grown bored. The troops
played cards, spread syphilis. Your wife
begged you to come back to Vienna.
Did you even notice when that Mr. Toplak
carried off your daughter? Your investment
had gone to Ptuj. When the messenger
brought the news that you disinherited her,
Baberle turned gray on the mountain road.
Dumbfounded she stared at her offspring.
She never understood the language of her children
raised by barbaric Slavic maids. It's written:
our mother lay down all white and kept
pressing the buzzer no one heard.
That's not the way you figured it, *mon général.*

Man with the Golden Eye

I remember the nun who studied in the Jagiellonian
library in Kraków. I was sad. Outside there were
sled tracks in the snow. In my thoughts I was
somewhere far south. I ate peanuts out of their shells.
Yesterday I saw the feathers of Montezuma
and how he longed for his ruin, for some foreign
god to drink up his soul. The Empire is eternal.
Eternal are the mirrors. The water evaporates,
only the gaze remains. Who hoards it?
A chariot with a golden shaft?
I'm not that yellow fruit.
I'm not that mob staggering from the Coronation.
I ate the ticket to the Anthropological Museum
while I spoke to a tourist,
while I kept looking at you.

The Boat

Genesis is tiny silken
shifts, thinner than
the nail of your little finger. Are earthquakes and wars
the collapse of galaxies? A couple of swipes
with a brush at the earth's skin,
a diary?
What is minimal?
What proves
the madness of a bud opening,
of a deer grazing? The poet bestows
wreathes, lays on hands. Yet only he who
veils his vision survives.
He who has seen too much has his eyes
pecked out by crows, and
rightfully so. The poet
kills the deer.

Small Wonder That Our Old Professor Is Now Mayor of Rome

I sat on a wall and sketched Perugia.
Argan also drops some coins in the almsbox.
For lunch at the *pensione* they give us cat meat,
at least that's what they say. I get better.
I'll never pass that exam.
Braco is in love with Vera, am I in love with Tatyana
or with Vera? Or with Dunya?
But not the Dunya who was in Perugia
and is an opera singer now, rather the Dunya
I was with at camp.
Vera and I saw each other in Greece.
Braco and I never saw each other at
camp. The English woman says
driving lessons here are practically free.
Tone will be the cause of our breaking up. Don't even
know how to use an eraser. In
Split Dikan stole Vera from me.
My surveyor abandons me in Orvieto.
I watch the people burning in hell.
They're naked and touching each other and then
they are included in frescoes and then Western
civilization clearly has nothing to point to
but a brothel
and in churches at that.

Marko

And just as I was
wondering whether our snake
was still alive —we had all been
worried, because it had been
a week since it had touched
any milk—the door bell rang.
On the stairway stood
a woman clutching at her
heart. "Marko doesn't have a father anymore."
I didn't understand. I thought about how
right I was to oppose
ash blue for the
door. You have to
insist, or there will be
scenes. At the top of the stairway Mother
appeared. I went
without a word straight to the basement
and the snake. I sat down on some
logs.
This snake will die, too, because I read too much
Proust. I decided to give up playing
the piano. To be
a better Boy Scout.
I've always wanted Yugoslavia
to win.

Epitaph

Only God exists. Spirits are a phantom.
Blind shadows of machines concealing the Kiss.
My Death is my Death. It won't be shared
with the dull peace of others laid beneath this sod.

Whoever kneels at my grave—take note—
the earth will shake. I'll extract the sweet juices from
your genitals and neck. Give me your lips.
Take care that no thorns pierce your

eardrums as you writhe, like a worm,
the living before the dead. Let this oxygen
bomb wash you gently. Blow you up only

as far as your heart will support. Stand up
and remember: I love everyone who truly knows me.
Always. Get up now. You've pledged yourself and awakened.

Light Not Fed by Light

Scent of flowering buckwheat,
why do you lure Transylvanian vampires?
Scissors are a painful tool.
No one has the right to crush a stone,

move a doorway from east to north.
But still the archaeologists find forged
iron. How to crush responsibility?
Unchecked, it grows into pandemonium. The creature that

first stared into a fire was fried—
the flame was terrible even in the rain—
and it wanted the fire for itself. Fate is in desire.

The trees burned blissfully. Whoever *saves*
his life will be spared. Only the one who
splits the mirror with a diamond can sleep soundly.

One, My Arm

The Holy Ghost came down and kissed me.
Far, far off I hear an avalanche.
My fingers go roaring through a jungle.
A fig tree is growing in this room.

My chest has gone all pink.
My eye is black.
A peacock's tail is growing out of me.
I am the Buddha.

What will become of the horses in the Russian steppe
when the charred honey starts to flow!
The bright fluid circulates in the earth's flower,
its blossoms contained in green pipes.

Mountains and non-mountains squeezed in one,
my arm, I am in stardust.
My face licked, by whom,
a deer, a cat?

I am
dew in a can which
a child can carry,
I am sweet white milk.

Memory

In the cry
of heaven I hear
the deadly

silence
of birth
impressing itself

on people and
animals. I
rave in

the snow. My
tracks water
the mind

of the masters.
An insect slices through
the air and

leaves.

[untitled]

With my tongue,
like a faithful, devoted
dog, I lick Your
golden head,
Reader.
Terrible is my
love.

Paris, 1978

Europe's heart is elegant and
dead. Only the children
still tremble before time
crushes them. We're torn between two
greater planes—Satan, the institution
of the entryway and the overhang
of freedom, which runs into
the Pacific. But we
are memory. And hence responsible
for the world, although our myth is built into
a machine we no longer control.
Our only real historical chance is
grace, which we alone are helpless to
bestow or set in motion.
Psychoanalysis is the bottom, the night
before the revelation.
All the laboratories of power
will collapse.

Pour un jeune Chalamoun qui se vend dans la rue

Powerful white teeth!
Membranes that enter the village of my eyes like
swords. I want your soul, to give it
to mine. I'm tired of
taking, I'd rather give myself.
Tu te rends compte? Am I to rent another
loft to dry our souls? This hotel
practice is costing me
enough already. I'm a professional and so are
you, only your trade is blank paper.
Every sheep, every cow is capital.
And I want my own sheep, my own
cows, not those stinking beasts
Alsatian peasants own. My animals are
history, because they give milk. But
you throw your paper away so that
store windows smell of your soul, which is
exuded from your books, as though they were some kind
of apple. Okay, give me your body for free, but this will
cost you. My job is not to
give my soul, just to take the money and not
give my soul.

The Right of the Strong

The right of the strong is to take everything.
Memory and youth, clouds and
melancholy. I didn't know,
I swear I didn't know what I was doing,
robbing all of you of your hearts. I was
just happy, moved and grateful to my
bright stars. I thought my loot was
love, and dust, mute now,
a gift. I raised many
species. Winged monkeys and
sky-blue cockatoos. Even you,
foxes, I lured over, so you became
the king among beasts. I truly thought I was
a holy ant that brought it all
on its own shoulders. Therefore now
I rot deliriously, waiting for the hour
you, meadows, will turn green. With
the erasure of my body the seal will be
returned to you. Crickets and brooks, sunrise
above the Trenta valley. The soft
mists above home will again be
sacred, as they used to be.
Just a while longer, poisoned children. Just
one more sip before I return
to earth.

[untitled]

Who should we call? The space, the people
are wiped out. Guns didn't help it,
it was too poorly armed to defend
itself. The enemy grew up in its heart
from inside. Out of hatred for itself,
out of hatred of its own freedom,
out of hatred—like the panic on the staircase,
so typical of servants when a storm
is rising—for the master of their envy and a few
crumbs it had grabbed to cure
its dead soul. Nameless bastard,
bastard with your bagmen, how do you
propose to legitimize yourself to me? Do you think
you're better because I speak a language
outwardly like your own? I was right
from the start. You were destroyed
from within, the blood flowed out nowhere. Deafness
and silence are your gestures, the indistinct gurgling
of strangled infants and aborted dreams.
Look, you've been tossed off, soundlessly obliterated, and
no one even noticed. I recall the
liberation of Ljubljana, yours and mine—
ours—the nervous smoking of the
Russian on the balcony, the speeches by the poet and the
condottiere, the sweetheart of the air that then
proceeded to corrode his vital organs, as it
had the man from Vrhnika and everyone who couldn't
pay the 60 goldeners for passage
to Vienna. In 1910. In
1974. Incompetent, except for filming
liquidations, ludicrous flicks of pathetic
deaths, fruit rotten from birth, expected to
fertilize these rocks. With what seed? Land

without god or sea. What use to you is the house if it
sits empty and dead, what use are the screams of victims you've
publicly tortured in collective frenzy, an obsession
to save yourself? Vampire,
bloated anniversary of deaths, sub-
alpine cornucopia of gilded altars. That's it exactly.
As in rustic baroque churches, or Chile. You and
I have less in common than the dirt
under my fingernail. Here, have your language back.

Gesture

I drank mead, wider than a river.
Dragonflies kissed my eyes.
I was weaving linen that became ice.
A ruined city glitters in it.

Streets are leading and aren't leading anywhere.
Leaning against a wall they sleep dead dreams.
And a muleteer's arm is raised the way it was
back then, when he shouted to the boy: Hurry!

We must reach the gate before sunset!

Functions

To want is to rub out death.
To smack its white skin with a stamp
and then stare at the eggs.
Spin a vase around, let it hiss like a top,
and dismember hymns.
Nature contains several planes,
one of which walks balanced on edge, munching milk.
To want is to collapse into ocean galleys.
To sizzle blows.
Spill wine on a tray and wash your
hands in it.
Wanting is the head's powerhouse, not the heart's.
Hunger of desiccated fish, perishing in steam boilers.
A lone grape drops every minute.
Shoulders broaden.
To want is to remove the black cross from around a peasant's neck.
To sing in meadows, call in the void.
To brush against blood's horns and shove them, shove them.
Under the sun, the home of bile, our discus is bile.
To want is to breathe.
To peel moss off a carpenter's axe with your hands.
To blow, blow hard.
To singe meat, cut into cubes, so its head turns black like a cricket's.
Trees hold amber, people don't.
To want is to sleep—sleep and forget about everything.
The shafts are beautiful.
Hay on a cart is the enemy of mankind.
Long-bearded peasants are asleep on it,
clutching pitchforks to their belts.
To want is not to smoke.
To cross your arms on your chest and think of the Arno.
You were greater than the Danube.
To want is to count your brothers, there are so many.

To run through a checkpoint with your head down and let out a
        whoop
of freedom.
Four people quarter it on a chair.
It wanders the world like a breed and dies out,
with dark hoops around its loins.
To want is to fade with the beeches, vines and maples.
Rub snow into your shoulders.
To stand and wave at trains and cry like
people chained to flight.
To want is to greet a worm and show it respect.
To pour brandy on your knuckles.
To want is to tear up the sun, crumble it in your hands
like a dirt clod.
Pile high coat upon coat, sheepskin on
sheepskin, dead.
Break necks at power plants and fall asleep like a blossom.
Let it sleep, let it sleep.
Let it wilt in a spasm of madness.
Tribes perform circle dances on the black wadding of corpses.
Let the skin run through my veins like
banknotes through the blood of Indians.
To want is to break a storm, pour
diamonds into coffee.
To seize the dance.
Seize each dancer separately.
To want is to listen coldbloodedly to hailstones
killing hamsters.
To climb up on a rocking chair and close your fingers around all
the babies that have died as sperm.
To grow a shadow.
To grow a shadow as rabble grows a cloud.
To slit the skins of drums.
To sleep, to fall asleep.
To want is to scrape salicylate off rulers.
To fall, to fall.

To stare grape pickers in the ear and
call them here.
We know little, I know little.
An upturned palm knows more.
To want is to scrape away the time.
Let girls with stones in their hands sew it
back up.
Hey, Pythagoras! Snot-nosed brat!
Artemis's little white coat got puked on.
To want is to wring a bird's neck so that it never
sings again.
To mount a pillar instead of a window and listen
to explosions in the distance.
To want is to have all your limbs smashed against the rocks.
The door bends in front of the field.
God only hears the diluted magma, nectar.
To want is not to notice when you put on your shoes
for the last time.
To want is to joke so much that scorpions
get caught on their bright, shiny
stingers, until they're finally preserved in bronze.
To want is to consent to death.

Schooling

I live wherever God wants me to.
Don't really have any will of my own, that's
nonsense, it's nonsense to talk like that.
God burdens me with all these encounters.
If I have a will, then it's like an old wooden fence: rotting.
Or we burn it, that's right, we burn it.
Sometimes I spend hours watching the fire in the chimney.
The fire is my brother.
Sometimes I inhale and nearly scream with madness.
But quietly, silently, quietly, so the pleasure's that much greater.
The air's my brother.
But my most horrible brother is my
body, and that's me myself.
I'm my own brother.
I have plenty of sisters, raindrops.
My sisters get me all wet.
I'm living in heaven now, because I got it out.
I cry because there are people who don't want to live in heaven.
It's harder to find a human being than a gold mine.
Sometimes I think if I got them all wet they'd all run to heaven.
So I soak them, and they go to heaven, but then they fall out.
Some people say I've chopped their arms
off, just because my arm is moving.
They're doing me wrong.
It pains me to think I kill.
Sometimes I think they've all killed themselves, to spite me.
I visit their graves.
They don't resent me.
They sanctify each person who has killed.
But I'm light and buoyant.
When I die, I'll be even fiercer.
Sins are my allies.
Sometimes I throw a scarf on my head.

Then I pace up and down like a tiger in a cage.
When the time comes, the chains will burst of themselves.
An airplane picks me up and off I go.
Wherever I wind up, I kiss the earth.
Today the Pope mimics me.
But popes are dolts; I only think about
Christ.
That's why I don't like feeling sweaters on my skin.
This dead sheep hurts, it hurts.
But I'm made differently than Christ.
Sometimes Christ really gets on my nerves.
They buried him in a field.
The field doesn't yield cinders anymore —
I provide the cinders.
I always moisten my bread with tears.
But Christ gave up crying.
If the two of us were swimming in the ocean, I'd dunk him.
Which one of us has a better crawl stroke?
Who dove best off the Menorca cliffs?
That boy who was twenty years younger?
He was underdeveloped.
His parents didn't send him to the better schools.
I'm amazed when I meet such
young people who don't know how to swim fast.
It seems to me the parents are to blame for that.
I carried him on my shoulders and threw him in
the water, so he would learn how to dive.
Christ also wore a sheep on his head.
But Christ was inundated with icons.
I pound on the frescoes and howl.
I lack presence of mind.
But the limbs he throws away grow back.
Why didn't they eat his flesh when it was still
fresh!
When I die, my flesh will be sweet.
And if you don't eat it then, I'll set myself on fire,

now!
I want you to eat everything I create, even
if it makes you vomit later.
I've seen people who vomited and
dreamed they had killed me.
My friends wanted to slit my veins.
But God has been my friend all His
life, so I escaped.
Now I wait for some tragedy to occur.
Tragedies calm me.
Tragedies open doors.
So now I sit and smoke, calculating as I write.
My kindness chews through animals' windpipes.
There are nothing but monsters in God.
There are monsters in God because the world is underdeveloped.
The world bursts when you open it, like an egg.
There's always some sperm or other on my body.
I should take a look at my sperm.
I see such gardens that the people
near me begin to lose their minds.
When they start to lose their bearings and collapse,
I know I'll be writing soon.
To me, people are puppies nipping at themselves.
Daisies never nip at themselves.
Daisies are fixed in the ground, but I like anything that
moves.
A daisy only moves when one of its petals
falls off.
The petals fall into my blood!
I'm a daisy petal!
A lynx, turf, a spider, gold, a clock, death,
father, mother, baby, old man, a wall, a frog,
a crust of bread, the wind, a whip, earth's whiteness,
spearhead, water lily, a wire, aura, the north, whatever
has cabbage in its head, tormenter and victim,
a blackbird, bucket, bridge, a sifter, apple, bread,

the crust of bread I throw away, a head, a seal,
a cylinder, a tree, a flash, a bee, a mountain,
a tiny baby, a slightly bigger baby,
dew, Mardi Gras, the balcony, a drum, power
preening as it eats.
I'm a constant geyser.
I raise them so they'll write about me.

Whale, Whale, Stay Alone!

A cow, does it suffer if you stab the calf
in its belly? Does a river suffer if you dry it up? And
balsam, does it suffer if you let it dry alone and yellow
in a box instead of putting it on your skin? Crowds do not
suffer, because there are many of them. They crowd together
and spread a bad smell. They look into each others'
eyes and know: we are dying like humiliated shit.
How could I be moved by that! Yes, if someone in a crowd
becomes a king and is then killed! Or
if a king becomes poor and has to use wood
sparingly. Things like this move me.
But as far as crowds go, they are covered
with rancid butter that poisons my blood. All whales
are stupid. I have proof.

The Fish

I am a carnivore, but a plant.
I am God and man in one.
I'm a chrysalis. Mankind grows out of me.
My brain is liquefied like
a flower, so I can love better. Sometimes I dip
my fingers in it and it's warm. Nasty people
say others have drowned
in it. Not true. I am a belly.
I put up travelers in it.
I have a wife who loves me.
Sometimes I'm afraid she loves me
more than I love her and I get sad and
depressed. My wife breathes like a small
bird. Her body soothes me.
My wife is afraid of other guests.
I say to her, now, now, don't be afraid.
All our guests are a single being, for both of us.
A white match with a blue head has fallen into my
typewriter. My nails are all dirty.
I'm thinking hard now what to write.
One of my neighbors has terribly noisy
children. I am God, I calm them down.
At one I'm going to the dentist, Dr. Mena,
Calle Reloj. I'll ring the bell and ask him
to pull my tooth, because it hurts too much.
I'm happiest in my sleep and when I write.
The masters pass me along from hand to hand.
That's essential. It's just as essential as
growing is for trees. A tree needs earth.
I need earth so I won't go mad.
I'll live four hundred and fifty years.
Tarzs Rebazar has been alive six hundred.
I don't know if that was him in the white coat,

168

I still can't make them out. When I write I have
a different bed. Sometimes I start pouring out more like
water, because water is most loving of all.
Fear injures people. A flower is softest
if you close your hand around it. Flowers like
hands. I like everything. Last night I
dreamed my father leaned across toward
Harriet. Other women frighten me, and
so I don't sleep with them. But the distance between
God and young people is slight.
There's always just a single woman in God, and that's
my wife. I'm not afraid of my guests tearing
me apart. I can give them anything, it will just grow back.
The more I give, the more it grows back. Then it launches off
as a source of help for other creatures. On some planet
there's a central storehouse for my flesh. I don't know
which one it's on. Whoever drinks it will
be happy. I'm a water hose. I'm God, because
I love. Everything dark in here, inside, nothing
outside. I can X-ray any creature.
I'm rumbling. When I hear the juices in my
body, I know I'm in a state of grace. I would have to
consume money day and night if I wanted to
build a life, and still it wouldn't help. I was made to
shine. Money is death. I'll go out on the terrace.
From there I can see the whole countryside as far as Dolores
Hidalgo. It's warm and soft as Tuscany,
though it's not Tuscany. Metka and I sit there,
watching. Her hands are like Shakti's. My
mouth is like some Egyptian beast's. Love is
all. Moses's wicker basket never
struck the rocks. Miniature horses come
trotting out of the level countryside. A wind blows
from the Sierras. I slide headfirst into people's
mouths and kill and give birth,
kill and give birth, because I write.

Home

Far away where the meadows are dark,
A dry flower grows speckled with snow.
The rooster crows, although it's winter,
Struts, his feet like hooves.

Far away where the rose blossoms in the snow,
Blue rose on white snow,
The sun embraces her and rocks her to sleep,
Love protects her from the shadow of a tree.

Far away where cascades roll over the rocks,
Where the mountain goats guard the grass with their bodies,
There's a bridge. I stand on that bridge.
I don't know whether to jump, or go for a swim.

The sound of spoons can be heard round the house.
Smoke, white smoke in the clear sky.
It smells of bread, it smells of cornmeal.
The little girl opens the window for the birds to eat.

Far away in the juniper forest there are many colored ribbons.
The trees are snowbound and there are no sleds.
The ribbons tear and fly like kites
So that you may rest your head on the blue of the sky.

To the Traveler

A flower slid down my shoulder
and fell in the water.
People whispered:
why didn't you catch it?
And the town bell tolled in farewell
as if saying goodbye to me.
But I wasn't fooled.
I drew the flower in the grass
and kicked the boat away from me.
Then I took the bugle in my hand,
its golden sugar cube
that melted in the sun.

Rabbit Oaxaqueño

Rabbit reading the Bible,
Why does your mother read the Bible too?
Why do you live in garbage, rabbit?
Where did you get these mirrors?

Rabbit, why are the children on the road boxing?
Rabbit, how come the children on the road have boxing gloves?
Rabbit, how come your mirrors are six feet tall
and only a few inches wide?

Why don't you have a chair, rabbit?
Why don't you have a table?
Where do you wash your face, rabbit?
Where is your water?

Hey, *oaxaqueño!*

Rabbit hugs me and falls asleep.

Black Madonna

In Mexico there's a Madonna with her teeth ajar.
A snake makes its garden there.
Her red mouth is not a real mouth.
Her mouth is red varnish.
The candles burn underneath the Lord Christ.

The Lord has a head skewered
with hair-tufts like a doll.
If you could only see his trousers made of banners,
violet trousers with golden tassels.

Between the violet trousers and golden tassels
there are fingerprints of nuns.
Nuns. Flies. Nuns. Flies.
   How should I know what they are?

Between the violet trousers and golden tassels
the Indians slide
on their knees!
They kick the wooden benches
with the soles of their feet.
They butt into the wooden benches
until they collapse.

Sonnet About Milk

Lord, I discovered milk, my bloodthirsty
milk in a gray saucepan on the stove!
Those waist-high gushing dairy hoses
outside the window are the source of my unhappiness.

If I beat it, it boils. If it boils, it overflows.
How to accustom oneself to this white madness.
It hates its own shape and takes that of a pan.
I'm watching Daniel building a house for us

under the window without really seeing him.
Today is Friday, March 7. I've eaten everything:
cauliflower, soup. Nothing left for the guests.

Nothing, absolutely nothing. As the milk rises,
my rubber soles squeak on the cement floor.
I should have changed shoes long ago.

The Tree of Life

I was born in a wheat field snapping my fingers.
A white chalk ran across the green blackboard.
Dew made me lie on the ground.
I played with pearls.

I leaned fields against my ear, and meadows.
The stars were crackling.
Under a bridge I carved an inscription: I don't know how to read.
They rinsed the factories with salt water.

Cherries were my soldiers.
I was throwing gloves into the thorn bushes.
We ate fish with the golden break knife.
In the chandelier above the table not all the candles were burning.

Mother played the piano.
I climbed on my father's shoulders.
I stepped on white mushrooms, watching the clouds of dust,
Touching branches from the room's window.

Prayer for Bread

He, who will not know how to drink the miracle,
will burn down. It is that powerful. And he,
who in the miracle won't grasp the soil like a bulldozer,
will be like the feather a bird discards.
We are humans, not flowers.
Their tranquility blossoms only out of dead flesh,
so let's not run ahead of time.
The spirit never loses itself in haste,
which, if it runs ahead empty, returns.
I am a circle until I become power.
And if I hurt your face,
hit your screams when you sleep,
if I dispossess you over and over like the poison
of chaos,
then kneel like a sacred animal
that just finished nursing.
Kiss the ground and cast
a curse on me.
Chain me down with your hatred,
so I can crush you into
love.

The Power of the Oeuvre

I am a stone.
The bottom of pain which the moon shines on, not the sun.
I am the train that has come uncoupled.
People have stopped waving to it from the platform.
I am the hay set on fire
to stir your hunger.
Attention is obliterated.
I am smoke.
A broken smoke ring, bluer than
plankton which devours the sea's color, if it does glow.
My chest is crumpled.
The horses are walled in.
A river peeling off its water
dries out the bed it flowed through.
A seed that grows is a dead spell over the earth.
Since wherever an oak grows there cannot
be any more delicate
mists or rustling of maple leaves.
The carpet running through the drawing room is red.
And the noble color of the parquet floor
is brutally covered with the product of human hands.
The blood of slaughtered sheep is there,
which is why we tread on it so softly
till the breathing of their lives
destroys us.

Lapis Lazuli

Three nights in a row I spent among the gnostics.
White butterflies hunted each other above the roses
while the snakes writhed and swallowed each other.
Here, it's just like over there. People are born and die.

We put hands on their heads. Only the hair of my friends
grew thicker there. Will the human race go bald?
I met lynxes who told me they came from Dacia.
Muhammad was absent. That's why there was a hole

in the belly of the earth. Amazing
voluptuous curves! Lumps of flesh
permeated with the spirit and an infinite number of ships
with white sails. Are they sailing for oil?

One shouldn't imagine that the sects were kinder
to each other. The Communists ate the monkeys
and the monkeys threw bananas at kings. Hat and pot were one
and the same thing. I remember how that first night

I cooked the meat on the stone not realizing
I could be using my hat. Now I get it!
What our hair lacks is oil. Who still piles up stones
around trees! The water still

makes a lot of noise while it flows, and the skin
still glows powerfully. And the train that rushes
out of the body into the heart
makes frightened lizards leap off its rails

so that a purple cape almost covers the sky.
No way, I say! It's blue. I turn from my back to my stomach
and shoot at the sky. The earth, the faces, the loves
that passed through my life, everything turns into lapis lazuli.

Sky Above Querétaro

Who are the beings dimming now
in the black heavens
who have the smell of rat kings?
Pearls jingle in vases
and the rose would jump like a frog,
if she were not tied.
Are the stars a burden?
Is water the fruit of millions and millions of years of labor?
The crystals do not change.
You can't catch a rabbit with your bare hands.
The paint has peeled from the cathedral wall
onto the cart of the ice-cream vendor.
Who are the beings who halt my steps and make the leaves rustle?
The keys tinkle
hung by the rope of dew.
Is that the king of the rats himself
who's slipping me the symbols and the hours?
Isn't he buried in the black earth like King Matthias?
My cart doesn't have a beard.
The stone slabs of my table are falling apart like the Conquest.
And again an orange appears in heaven
which piously and quickly I make spin
to stretch and pluck at its petal,
and—

does the earth continue to breathe then?

Cantina in Querétaro

I see a horse who cries when he meets the eyes of another horse.
You are brothers: the angel with the apple, the cataract of the
    underworld.
The sun on your manes is for both of us.
Why do you tear me apart, jealous stallions?
Horses are holy beasts! You are both César Vallejo.
Enormous quantities of spirit and flame flow through us.
Is it possible for the genius of the dead poet
to divide itself into two rivers, tear apart like a handkerchief?
You are one symbol, bread for the masses.
My two arms are both of equal length.
My two legs belong to everybody.
My kiss is not a shackle. Look!
This is the pneuma which Jakob Böhme breathed,
still virginal, which I carry in my breast
the way women from Kras carry water pitchers on their heads.
However, if I still have to listen to the petty bourgeois problems of
    the Nicene Council
and witness the liquidation of cadres tested in guerrilla warfare,
then you my little stallions will have to go back again,
march forward into the dark.
In this cantina, others might know how to stick knives into you
while I calmly drop the small coins
por mi copa de alma blanca.

For David

It's evening.
The birds perch on the branches with a racket, and
I think:
if I were my son,
would I thumb through my Larousse before I
spoke, too?
Would it hurt him?
Would I wonder at this clatter?
Ride a horse in the Sierras, young?
Shudder, looking at godlike forms?
A green T-shirt,
violet sweater,
the arch made by the line between the pane and
metal door frame—glimpsed through the window
of that fearsome craftsman, Maya —
on my terrace?
Would Robert also visit him,
drink beer and talk about
planting trees out in the country
where it rains incessantly and the
waves of the Pacific break against the rocks?
Does the soul grow with the body?
Didn't the Minotaur keep its legs stretched out?
For if the scent should leave us,
how could we ever be tracked down by the gods—
creatures just as
frail and gentle as ducks and our distant ancestors.

Nihil est in intellectu...

Here's how I know God:
the taste of a ripe pear or that
silken explosion of the air that
sinks in, spewing empty
blueness.
Head and hair are washed clean instantly.
I'm afraid that—let's say,
your eyes—will melt
onto my hands,
exude a fragrance toward the sky or thunder to the netherworld like
the falls along the Savica.
And I always hear a fluttering of flags,
a glorious crunch, like the Titanic
sinking, a chicken
being torn apart.
And when all this happens—
I give you my seal—
I give you back your everlasting purity.
For only they are sad who never
have been ripped apart.
Sí, que te veo como un Dios, Hombre!

Turtle

Turtle alone can with its poisonous
geography and hard shell nurse
the star.
The star, where soya grows
on the parallel, green sky,
while all the soldiers of the world
try to swallow saliva
and never can.

Turtle with its terrible dynamite
and the bridal veil is like
a couple! a couple!
renewing the Mother
from destroyed milk,
rolled over by tanks.

Turtle alone with its artful
head and watery sounds
—the earth's back is turning—
kills and holds back death,
and sweetness in a mouth
shakes itself and is born.

The cross you can undress
and it wouldn't be aware of it.

Only turtle erupts Memory.

To the Deaf Ones

I've grown weary of your vapid skies.
Leg touching leg, lips to lips, all dead.
What is this power preventing a flowering?
A gulag in toadies' heads, spreading like cancer?
I carry God in my heart, give Him away
like water to people dying of thirst,
who languish from imagined provincial
tectonics and the pedestal of a suicide,
the national hero.
Weak-kneed, murderous, drowsy,
no longer feeling fear.
I refuse to be free
everywhere else, and fall into a soulless black
void only in my native land.
I'm not a cynic, I'm a poet, a prophet.
I go off with my life to the place where I am.
Your nets won't strangle me, and
your Sainte-Beuvian gibberish is
a criterion for no one.
I refuse to trip and fall like Cankar.
They won't gild me into a sterile catechism like they did to Župančič.
The sea is my element, and if you don't have it, I'll give it to you.
The air is my element, mortified and poisoned,
now purified.
Even if I'm the only one breathing freedom,
I won't give in.
I'd sooner choose death than the humiliating genocide of your
breakfast preserves.
The soul is eternal, haven't you heard?
It was me who told you that.
This space will survive only
by some tremendous effort of us all.
And if you insist on getting underfoot,

I'll trample you like ants.
Better one live soul that can tell of its ecstasies and
torments than this clotted gelatin
of a Hades, not even the shadow of a trace
of the living people and straightforward
time that breathe beneath this very
earth, above this sky. You
just need fangs, you
must strike with the grace of gods
at the heart of this ramshackle destiny, so that
someone will wake up and hear.

Gracias a la vida, que me ha dado tanto!

Death's Window

To stop the blood of flowers and rotate the order of things.
To die in the river, to die in the river.
To hear the heart of the rat. There's no difference
Between the moon's and my tribe's silver.

To clean the field and run as far as the earth's edge.
To carry in my breast the word: the crystal. At the door
The soap's evaporating, the conflagration lit up the day.
To turn around, to turn around once more.

And to strip the frock. The poppy had bitten through the sky.
To walk the desert roads and drink shadows.
To feel the oak tree in the mouth of a spring.

To stop the blood of flowers, to stop the blood of flowers.
The altars look at each other, eye to eye.
To lie down on a blue cabbage.

Light for Hamdija Demirović

Ahac had an esteem for the Piedmont folk.
They were the only truly courageous
Italian partisans. The word cannot afflict me
lethally, it cannot. Not even the night
and even less the solitude. Nevertheless. If I were to
kill myself, I would, dying, write with my blood
Cesare Pavese's lines from *Lavorare stanca*. Not my lines,
which don't even reach to his knees.
I feel like a wild animal now, crawling on
Cesare's breast, its teeth beginning to
dig a grave in his blood, very close to the heart.
I would drink up his loneliness and then die.
I would die my own and his own death. For both of us.
What more can art do? To count out the ships?
The eye is resting on the blue sea-level, counting.
It translates into fingers. I'm writing
what I have seen. I love the good heart of
Cesare Pavese. The touch of his blood makes me
bronzelike. The smoke twines toward the sky
from the burning grass. How wrong are those who think
I will not kill myself.

Light-blue Pillow

It was all happening inside a huge light-blue
pillow, inside some kind of rattle they give
to the newborn, and which was named light-blue
pillow since that's the name I found for it
in my dream. It was hollow and full of light,
so that it was larger than the largest hall,
including Albert Hall and Lincoln Center.
All the way up near the ceiling there was a junk
approximately two stories high and fenced
by dark-gray palisades. Perhaps it'd be better to call it a gondola?
I stood on the ground floor between sculptures.
I was with people. There we will dine, I said
to my companions, who nodded their heads.
But already we were carried down the stairs
into the depths below where some other people
were engaged in disco dancing on the floor of bronze.
They showed great discipline and nervousness.
Our gestures were identical with theirs until
we were carried through a swinging door no bigger
than the distance between the knee and the chin.
The music ceased completely on the other side,
although there was no wall or soundproofing.
I heard only the humming of bees. Our position kept changing.
Again, in the distance, high under the ceiling,
there was the junk. Again I pointed in its direction.
There we will dine, I said to my companions,
who again nodded their heads.

The Hunter

Somehow I know, I know these things,
like when I will have a shepherd's
bad luck, always the horrible creed
of the hunter, and my heart starts to bleed.

High in the air the billowing shouts
mean nothing at all, even
if I, the swindler, don't manage
to fill myself with my own dark powers.

In the dark blue brightness,
my desire expands into the sweet
ozone, ecstasy is a precise gait,
I am where I am, and in the room.

Then the victim collapses,
and I replace suns.
I eat and shiver, my soul
can never get enough from a

jar made like this. My mouth
begins to water.
Just ordinary
spit, not blood, because the sweetness

of these white explosions,
these miracles in the air, hurts.
The same passion in a flower, in an avalanche
of this image, as among gods.

To Read: To Love

As I read you, I swim. Like a bear-bear with paws,
you push me into bliss. You lie on top of me, who
tore me apart. You I fell in love with unto death, first
among the born. It took but a moment and I was your bonfire.

I am safe as never before. You are the ultimate
feeling of fulfillment: to know where longing comes from.
I'm in a soft grave whenever inside you. You cut, you illuminate,
every layer. Time bursts into flame and disappears. I hear hymns

when I watch you. You are strict and demanding, concrete. And I
cannot speak. I know I long for you, hard grey steel. For one of
your touches, I give up everything. Look, the late afternoon sun

is dashing against the walls of the courtyard in Urbino. I have died
for you. I feel you, I use you. Torturer. You uproot and you torch me,
always. And into the places you have destroyed, paradise flows.

Alone

We are one body, one breath.
We are three. Now, an empty bellows, me.

It hurts, the cliffs and guts give way.
Your compressed lips don't relax.

In vain! You don't lose!
Elsewhere I'll pulsate for your bright bombs.

I am true to you. Only hunger moves.
Your ground snow and dust.

I Lovingly Keep Watch

I had the seven rivers. All of them
were headless. I breathed out smoke. And
the sky, the nut trees, the dark and anxious
movements of my wildlife seemed
forlorn. I felt I was saving
someone. The moon was new. I clung
to a red ball. Roots
began to crunch, as under snow.
My body, though, was warm, contained
in two sun beams. The village
sank into the sky. I thought
I could skim my weight. And
he awoke. His eyelids beginning
to touch the line of life.

The Wheel

Oh, like a little puppy on the floor I slept
and washed myself in the window.
I did not believe your sweet heart.
We had breakfast, you
breathed like father time,
mortally dangerous to me.
I tied you down.
You forbade me to steal the horses.
They'll come on their own!
They'll come on their own!
And I licked my lips.

Only you are here, for me to burn
and forget, my belonging.
Collapsing wet rusty houses,
how am I to rise.
How am I to drink off my draughts
in this thick, poisoned
sea air.
You broke your eyes yourself and extracted
the scent with your hoarse rattle, your
banal black moaning.
You give a damn what happens to me.

No More

I shove my soul like a huge hay cart!
Away from myself. Ninny! Get away from me!
At first I saw it as a red cattle car full
of livestock on the tracks at Doboj.
Surely it was someone else's soul,
because I couldn't budge it an inch.
And what would Plato be doing in Doboj, with a gun?
Oh, to be young again and have it fit in my shoe.
How I flung it around—my black shoe—in the morning
when I woke up. Braco was still snoring by
the window and didn't hear me flinging the black
shoe. Back then those trolleys on wires still
zipped through Ljubljana in my head, so I could take them
to work. Whoosh! a trolley drove past
Gradišče, and I tossed my soul into it like
wet dough. How far I could heave stones!
And flowers. Violet-gray wallpaper of flowers.
Flowers! Flowers! And now my head is bleeding
and I'll get a rupture from this damned hay cart!
It would be enough for a pyromaniac to light a cigar
and carry the flame to his eyes.

Trout

I ate trout in Ohrid, then squatted
on the pier and played with the line.
Okudzhava wore black pointy shoes.
He placed one foot on the wicker chair
and sang in a hoarse voice
that came out of his shoe
about the horror of suppressed people.
Communism is devouring the mammoth,
the mammoth is devouring the slogan.
I wanted to kiss the wooden chair
because van Gogh sat in it.
He leaned against it with his foot.
Van Gogh placed down handkerchiefs on it.
The hammers that are flying through the heavens
are named the firecrackers.
Light falls on the kneeling crowd.
Whoever drowns in the lake
won't find its bottom
but a burning oasis, burning like fata morgana
under the lake's surface.
The tree trunks curse their bumps.
The bird's wings melt into stalactites.
O Russia, when will you let your maidens
wear white wreaths?
The sun shines at the head of the table
directly into the face of gods and animals.

My Tribe

My tribe
does not hear
freedom anymore.

Does not recognize it,
does not see it,
when it's touched by it.

My tribe
thinks
the slow

killing
of their bodies
and souls

is natural.
Only at times
when for a moment

it is pierced
by something
resembling ozone,

resembling childhood,
it wipes its sweaty
forehead,

shakes
this nightmare,
these chains

from itself,
turns around
and falls asleep.

Man and Boy

He had decided not to go to the beach.
A carpenter saws, he's read his gnostics.
Children in blue jumpers are out on recess.
Arm rests on arm, the watch on a guidebook to Delos.

It's too close, it smells too much.
He's happy, but afraid he's in too deep.
If the body truly merges with another and twitches in pleasure
for long, something else gives way. And you're

left hanging in the air, alone. But now he just
squeezes his eyes shut, feels the warmth of limbs
and powerful arms. Tomás, you're so gentle,
but powerful as an oak. Through your

body I see Apollo and the giants,
their faces and eyes, their heads which
float on water on wind on platters.
You're warm and soft. You're the master of the night.

Help Me!

The stars are cutting.
Your glance makes my blood run cold.
You've drunk off my power to cast
a shadow.
The pain that keeps me from turning
to ice
throbs like a blind, tired
dog.
You've crushed me, now I can
no longer turn my head.
While you sleep, breathing deeply, I make my escape.
You've exhausted me.
I'll no longer resist you.
But before the last drop
is gone, I shall
lay hands on myself and turn
you into my own
monument.

The Blue Vault

With your silent, slender hand you put out stars.
You give my name away as a bee makes honey.
Bite into me! You ignite my eyes. A distant sea
of buffaloes in the green, ashen
air. The taste is replaceable, I'm not.
Nailed to the cross, I spend your fruit.
And look—every drop of my memory
is a pulsing of the arch, hardened now
into the miracle that the heavens are alive.
The animal gives way, kneels down, is touched.
You shake off the blow-weed's white down:
the mark on your breast will flare up for
no one. You have ignited my neck
with your silent, soft lips.

To a Hero of Our Time

Your head,
your hands,
your deathly slender sutures,
your gait,
your stem,
your fearsome crystal voice,
your weight and sin of omission.

You are: trembling and appetite.

You crush so you may feed
and kill so you may
quietly and more devoutly smell
your white reeds.

Inane Saturn,
from eyelid to eyelid you kindle a fire
then shove it aside, not letting
me collapse in its flames.

You remove death from my grasp
like food from an animal.

The Burning Bush

I eat ice cream at the Zocalo in Tlalpan.
So what if it's unsanitary, if I get germs from
amoebas? There are signs set out beneath the flowers: *yo soy tu*
vida, tu aire. But the rock is still warm,
even though it's late.
I've been out on foot all day, and now I'll rest.
I've walked almost every street in the vicinity, looking
for a place to eat. And everywhere are germs
hiding under the white tablecloths, and they scorch their way
into your brain. My head is fastened to my
shoulders. Flowers are planted in the earth.
My arms are fastened to my shoulders,
too. When I walked along the edge of
the sidewalk, I unfastened all my buttons.
I rolled one sleeve up very, very high.
There are hummingbirds at the Zocalo in Tlalpan,
and now I'll come down off the bench, so I can
squat. Sometimes, if you suddenly squat
.down, beauty emanates. It gives off a scent
like a juniper bush ablaze.
Why can't the smell in the mirror be seen?

Guilt and Passion

The city transit vehicles are green.
The moon is full. Look out! I've set a
trap for you. I'm fighting the greediness
of my own fatalism, not
yours. My pneuma rolls you through
spaces your senses cannot
perceive. I'm wounded. Look out! I see
far. What they whispered to you was true.
I am the master who disposes over
the glow of others. Look out! I warn
you. You fend off wounds because you
sleep in crystal. I give just to take back.
To open and penetrate you. To
pierce through the bottom of time, because it is right.

To Him Who Was Prohibiting Me His Name

To grow up. To burst open the sky.
To run in bows and arrows and floods.
To smell the hamster. To smell the hamster.
Here. To pry open the muzzle.

To have soft gray tentacles.
To suffocate. To suffocate.
To bet double or nothing
and take off buzzing.

The whimpering. With the small thread
to double-stitch together the red pile.
To knead the breath out of clay,
no more to awake.

Let the blood flow like malleable
little soldiers with skis on,
no more to be seen
since they were swallowed up by the door.

Birds

I dreamed that blood flowed from his mouth.
He lay on the sand and stared into the void.
All around us breathed the cliffs.
With my shoes on I stomped on him, crushing his
nose. It seemed to me the birds
feared him. They would not claw him apart
if the stream of blood was too thin. I broke
his neck at its nape. I made slush
of his ears and face. He squeaked,
soaked with sand. The sky
gave way and deepened. Birds began to
gather in flocks and come near.

Red Cliff

Gently, gently as you can,
as you hear, as you know.
Darkly, darkly as you fall,
as you shine and as you eat.

Let the flies return to their hive.
Up with your hands, golden city.
Helmets glint, the sun goes down,
the terraced gardens calming down

and cooling. And when you draw back
the oar to keep from denting the pier,
fear not. You won't hit a thing.
You'll be a church. You'll be cloth. It's how you are.

Pont-Neuf

You are my flower, my lips, my heaven.
Embrace in your glance the seven grains.
I bear them until I collapse.
Until another scent pervades the stairway.

My heartbeat, my breath, my grass.
The tenderest felon, red satin.
The window of the labyrinth will crumble you. My palm
picks you up, systematically, as glass soaks up color.

We live for murder. Putrid fruit washed up by the Seine.
And when I lean you up against the wall and look around
to see if someone's coming, you turn to crystal.
My traitor, prolonging my life.

The Measure of Time

O you who made possible pure joy!
Suffering and casting off, the silent sowing,
the mute poisoning of juices and cells.
Which betrays me, pulls the straps tight. More! More!
Who with cruel gentleness wrings out my death.
The thief is my Grail.
You who forgot about me.
Who broke my blood the moment
I entered you.
Identical monster.
You who know nothing about loss.
The only trave of pleasure that ever sets your
skin on fire
is in that millionth split of a second
when you're grabbing for
cash.
Only then do you tremble.
You who set fire and burn with your look.
You who smell of August hay.
What are you waiting for iron prince, my
Saturn is already leaving.
Squeeze!
Bite into your ecstasy and look up.
Everything wavers: the sea, the moon, and Li Po.
Don't look back, my beloved.
You for whom I felt the deepest devotion.
I'm telling you, don't look back.
You're the one and only.
Only your snow is the crystal, the wall.

Lips

Steely forehead. Steely forehead.
When the sun comes out, you'll have it quenched.
You feed with me among the sky's black chains.
The wasp and lamb are blue.
Crystalline the flame.

Steely forehead. Steely forehead.
You're alloyed and whiter than the dawn.
Under these eyelids my
climbing parties died,
my heartbeat stopped forever.

I've breathed you in to keep
from hurting you.
So that, as I carry you
across the chasms,
I cry you into the void.

Flame and flesh,
you're a phantom, the black rose.
You saw yourself, before you burned,
taut in the bow.
Your palate is a husk.

To a Golem

Lost in thought,
you came to watch me.
I'm like an olive branch—your face.
Houses are on fire in the sun.
The bridge is pasted together stone by stone
and the sky keeps gnawing.
The hands are seizing me.
I hear the motion of soft nibs.
Smoke rises out of me.
I evaporate into you, tasting your
fruit, passer-by.
The sheep scratches herself on the rock,
the windows are wiped in a dream.
Sweet rehearsing pours over me.
I'm folding your door latches.
I shuck the black, silky
festive hall of your warm breath,
the impermanence of your life.

Shepherd

The snow buried all the trees, all the trees.
I'm warming my numb hands on the fire beneath the sheepfold.
My sheep are dropping on their backs from cold,
bleating their milklike cries, on their backs.

I've been in the mountains for ages guarding
the Seven Lakes. How the buzzards hovered.
They slew my sheep one by one under the Cross.
My soot turned white under the dark blue

firmament. Snow and ice devour everything.
They all had their moment except me: my pleasures,
my piping, my valley. I've always been alone

with my cruel dog who gnaws my bag strap
to ease his hunger and warm himself,
to make the sheep stop their dismembering in the snow.

The Window

The wind has no soul, not even a body!
They're both there blowing in my face!
On my fingers the nails are black!
There are gods hidden in them!
When I die the flower will blossom!
Everyone leaves to others his own bliss!
We never wanted to be anything else
but steel girders sticking out of concrete!
The worst imaginable kind of fascism would be
if the soul belonged only to the living,
and not to the dust and stones!
Enormous labor went into steel girders!
The centuries of the ore lying under the earth
and the drawing closer of men toward her!
The roar of engines! Cattle that had to step
back before the trucks loaded with girders!
I hear the screech of trees that fell
for the sake of paper bags
so the gray powder could fill them!
Or the white...
And mixed with it water—the same way
that I mix some things with my spit!
Who says the chauffeur didn't dream!
And who says this fish, this musk beetle
is an animal!
In the world there are innumerable disturbances!
So many night watchmen, bacteriologists,
hands that fiddle with strange knobs!
Cans are karmas sold by merchants
for the people to eat them!
Train whistles are cradles!
Everybody thinks eyelashes are mortal
since they vanish behind our senses!

If they set themselves on fire above the gas range
they supposedly don't exist!
The woodpile as high as the Pantheon collapses.
The lotus opens.
The moles have no eyes.
And the criminal mentality —
roll the men in flour,
grind up frogs' legs with some matches,
light the flame—
revels in silk in the sands of the desert!

Happiness Is Hot, Splattered Brains

Whoever is truly cast in pure love
needs no heaven, let heaven go.
The body blossoms into a terrible silence,
walls and chairs awaken.

Parts of things were once human
members, too. My love,
your warm pressure on my temples
hurts so much.

It pushes me into a sacred circle, shrinking
and expanding. Its massive hand
gives, and then scatters me
into the bone white of night.

We're passers-by here, lost and
helpless. Color, weight and sex
dissolve. My waterfall is hurting. The white
drops remain, awakened into granite.

Only cliché is real. Nostrils
flare. Attacked, destroyed, revered
and licked. Like a stone's white, shiny
parts, which generations and

generations have licked with love.
It was given to them to worship.
To scoot on their knees like bugs.
To groan with the almighty passion of God.

The Deer

Awe-inspiring cliff, white desire.
Water springing forth from blood.
Let my form narrow, let it crush my body,
so that everything is one: slag and skeletons, fistful of earth.

You drink me, draining off the color of my soul.
You lap me up, like a fly in a tiny boat.
My head is smeared, I see how
mountains were made, how stars were born.

You pulled your brow out from under me. There I stand.
Look, in the air. Within you, drained, all
mine. Golden roofs bend up under us,

small pagoda leaves. I'm in silken candies,
gentle and tenacious. I funnel the fog into your
breath, and your breath into the godhead of my garden, the deer.

The Four Questions of Melancholy

I know. You're off to war now, off to trample flowers.
You'll have dusty apples in your mouth. You'll count
your steps. You'll be aware of all the drops bubbling
forth from under moss. I hear a siren. Like a pink

bow it falls across the mountain, and it boils, exciting
longing in others and the heavy black handfuls of silk pressed
under your shirt. Peasants will be making wine, trampling
grapes underfoot, singing songs and celebrating.

You lie down, head resting on your backpack, and contemplate
your massive shank. Water defines the contours. You
lie by an apple tree, beside yards and yards of felled
timber, stacked high for winter. Where is your rabbit?

What's in the backpack? Why are you chewing straw?
And why so sad? Shadows have consumed the valley
now, and the last train has hobbled off to Bohinj.
Have your Friulian neighbor put you on his tractor

and drive you up the mountain. And on the ridge the two of you
can settle back, compare the colors: pitch black by now
and fading blue. Does your snake still molt whenever
you're framed in light? When you gaze at the woods?

St. Moritz on the Park

I eat your heart with a spoon: like honey, pure honey!
It crackles like cellophane, like a waterfall, you're white in my blood.
Smeared on a deer's snout. My head, my neck and shoulders, clear
to my chest covered with your sweet sustenance,

a surface where streetcars turn around.
You're a text. A cautery. Thread after thread.
More! Get the cask on the raft! Bacchus! Bacchus! But where
did this snow-covered gate with the golden latch come from?

The angle moves under pulsations, a golden section.
A dark blue stop, the moment when the sky is
exchanged. I have more silk than butterflies. And
the Chinese, the Tyrrhenean, your Altaic sky.

Makalú, Makalú, contained within a tiny, sweet host,
you float in my geometrical pastry. Nourished,
as I have fed my captives. Whipped! A temple cloth,
a dam beneath the light. How deliciously subdued and sleepy!

I and Thou

Your lips have never kissed me, you've never
drunk snow. You melancholy moment, frigid
under these snowdrifts. Let me ask a cruel question—
do you still heat your igloo? I cast a spell on you

and tore your limbs off. And those creases deepening
in what was once a godlike brow, perhaps you've even lost
your right to them. You haven't hurt me more, you haven't.
Little mummy, aborted flower, the memory of you fades.

Oceans divide us, and you're jaded. The hard stone
hopeless, smeared with silicate. We shall yet make love,
and I shall grease those beehives yet. My desire has weakened

now, you've won, you are indeed a void. And I,
the tree-lined path of countless others, contain your red heart,
gone rigid, too. I have gurgled with happiness only in you.

Walls

A poet lies, a river flows, a woman breathes.
We speak the truth with blows, a breaking in
two. What's between pieces of bread when they break?
What's inside Warsaw burning?

And rings that touch the ground when people die?
In our cellar the potatoes have gone wild, sent out shoots.
Go sleep in the park, go sleep inside light
so it can incorporate you into its lustrous walls.

If you're wrapped in a blanket that was
just covering a steaming horse—
it rested, it was tired, worn
out—don't lose a second:

on the ground in the garden there is a single,
solitary pear for each one. From far off,
like a giant, like a flower I sense how I
grabbed and spilled it in the light.

I Am Your Soul, Your Dove

You burned me down and strewed me about.
You set fire to me and dismember me.
My flower is in your temples, those
round blue spheres of land on which
I die
and harden.

You strangle me: I fructify the earth, give rise to rivers.
Hummingbirds have blacked out the sun
with pain and passion.
You're a thief, and I'm your obedient captive.
I crack beneath your boot.

Step on me, step on me, crush and annul me!
Other bugs will have to drink, too.
Let me flood all of you.
Like the bottommost layers of compost, your spoils.
Your immense, shuddering empire, which you
bandy about like a lamb.

You who warm me.
You who have destroyed me in chains of jade.
Who am yours, only yours, who clench me
in your teeth.

You tear at me, as Africa was torn from India.
I am the Himalayas.
As long as you watch me, a shore of me.
As long as you smell me, a shore of me.
As long as you love me.
Mute.

Milina, *My Line*

I watched it filling and collecting. An eyewitness. I
ordered the pyramids built myself. I couldn't help it.
I shivered. And collided with your smooth silk, the might
of the two-headed. I fell into you like a captive, a flickering

horse with my life's last ardor. You're an eagle. In all the
plasma of your venerators I'm the one most deeply wounded,
most exposed. I caress your wet hands.
I will kill. Anything the silken split second of the delta

of time, your tenderness's pulsation wants and needs, I too desire.
You draw on and disembody me. I cloak myself and overflow.
Let the great deluge descend, sucking in mountain inns,

other rivers, breathing cliffs. I shall respond with a
prayer. With a terrible, searing fire, in order to serve
you. So your gentle scepter may break my neck.

Note: *milina* (Slovenian; pronounced me-lee-nah)—grace; mercy.

Christ at Hermes' Door

Your face is buried, ounces of ice looking out from the block.
Is that you? Do I need a model for God?
Sweet, sweet, both of us humble and sweet.
Gas gathers in our teeth.

So that we grow blue fangs.
Who is that rubbing sand along our lips?
You're a vase. My hands caress you.
Gray clay spinning on a wheel.

When I shape your mouth with my palm, it stays.
Explodes. Changes color. Summons red from gray.
Does the fire caress you? Would your nails reek if they burned?
I wrap you around my forehead. Your skin's a belt.

I think you're formed, maybe just a little hard.
You hold water.
Will it fizz in you?
Will petals of flowers float on the surface?

Will they veer away from the sides?
Rush toward them?
Cool off? Will you need me to smash you?
Will you still want to run down my hands like honey?

I'll carry you around on my shoulder.
Agree to all roles that are rustling, sweet and light.
You're the cream with which I summon cliffs from the earth's bowels.
I pull them out.

When all else has melted, they don't melt.
When vanilla and the liquefied wings of my wood
flow at the earth's core. We don't combust.

Our fangs are made for this unbearable heat.

We're exhausted.
Alloyed, united like elephant and oak.
O ear wax of the she-elephant!
Have I shoved you in it?

The Tree of Redemption

Anch'io sono stupito. Your clumsy
hands crackle like marshes. Like a billion
silver years with no cross beams.
No crown. No ground. Mushrooms, ships
(at least boats on the canals). Each of your
hairs is a separate curriculum vitae. Saw
them off and plane them. Or tie them in a braid.
At least cover them with a kerchief, cover them!
When you tip the bottle to your mouth, don't you feel
it might wreck you? Every star heats its branding iron.
Sheer naked force won't help you flay even cattle.
You have to know where to cut. Where to
load on your thoughts. How to direct smoke through a hose
and into the woods. Does the sky harden slightly
before it runs? Does it burst like a windowpane? Dusty
crystals conduct pain outward like a cobweb from
the center of power, and in fact a white
veined way digs out the hole in the middle, not
the blow of the object itself. It blows into the car.

The Sea Lasts

It is natural to describe knives as beautiful.
Wild is the power of blood. Time, running,
curtains of the ultimate limits are causing this deep passion,

the call for revelation. You are suffocating. In your
too-young, wet, immersion. The basics are useless.
This is not a critique. It is the beauty, the glory. No less

than his majesty, leaning on the rich softness of his coat.
We need him. Not the same way we need
the torsos of angels among bulls. With

chopped wings and helmets. No. Your face must
be exposed, your tan, fur, soft folds, the extremity
of the burning trunks of Saturn. History should go

to work for you, arranged in people, in light, and
in techniques of huge chunks of matter. I want
to see rivers waving at you. Your every limb

stuck in my throat. Let the blueness of choruses last,
of rocks, let it change, let it alternate. Let your skin
feel. What crowds experience,

what makes them accepted at Court.
Separates raindrops even in the air. On the right
and on the left. Everywhere. In rhombs, ellipses,

in satin Vico's boxes, in the sand
granaries the son is building. The human arm is
shaped after that. All that is needed

is to add a grain of lustre to it,

the only true kiss. It is the same shift as
the deluge of the Mediterranean. For exactly one

million years desert floor and then again masses
of water pouring through Gibraltar. A few hundred years
for the sea to level,

for us to use up our time. Powerful are
the tongs of melancholy. Soft touches
of its blueness shoot up, and the flame dies.

[untitled]

Hear me out, the world
is *not* in danger.
Just as the fingers of two hands
interlock, so we are cared for above.
Every color has been arranged
completely, harmoniously,
because love is unending.
There is no edge, no out side.
No dark hollows, no cold.
Everything is strictly for use
and for our mirror.
Love us, spend us,
feed us.
Life is a buzz.
The white birch tends its race.
Everything is terrible.

Litmus

The balance fading in desire's straight line
goes along my ridge, up there. It hibernates. Becomes
a kind of ice cream. Sure, but how did they kill

Sadat? Where did the fire come from that visited
Pascal? Or how is it that shivers can crush your spine
(do they strain it?) if you have the gift of sniffing out the right word,

buried at just the right angle? As though you'd excavate three inches
of the soil on this mountain. The rocks lie there
with a purpose. This sky's blueness binds

and gags. Like Beuys, and terrorists. Whiteness, little eyes,
blood, stench. What does a bee know of pollination?
Who upends the cosmic rake, so that it glints

like the most suggestive erotic hint, causing
a command to harden in your brain: grab the sketch
for yourself, set it on your chest, disassemble it,

like a child for the first time dismantling
a radio to see if gnomes live inside. The sketch
is soft as a cupboard made of green rubber. It burns on

the mountains like a wildfire. It strains honey
into your eyebrows, your spine. Elongates your fingers.
And when you lunge and grasp that furry paw,

we're here, right here, the world will stand still, having used me
as its pillow, as a soldier
on his side with a slightly more generous nose. Fine.

The Neck

Can you endure me? As you transfix me, causing
my wings to shudder. The juice should flow right out,
through you, and seep into the ground. I should be

hungry and aching. When you look back,
it will be pumping terror. Falling like dead islands.
The cancer on which lakes heal. All matter smells and

drowns in silk, but those are only disjointed parts,
me, whom you have missed. Everything one could
dare to preserve is with you. Inside you like a

gyre. Like your plaintive leather dreams and laments.
Like my plough. Your silence and despair. Whose
bleeding nostrils? The blue liquefied gas

circulating through your senses, more grimly
consistent than when cash evaporates? It's all
in you. My blood, my father, my forebear. Submerged

settlements. Mountains I've bent back, if not
pierced through. My scent, how it pervades
lush groves. How you seize spruce trunks,

withstanding their tar and coarseness. Your neck,
oh how I wring it, and you scatter the pleasure
down through your body. The sphere hums.

And what of your velvet's gray-scaled softness? That
water so suited to your eyes and mine that it flows
over. Causing two rustlings to lunge at, grapple,

embrace each other, two forces that set out and
order the sky like a peasant stacking timber. That
rump, grunt, and tear, until it explodes. Sticks to itself.

So that it's soaked and bound. So that silent machines
like black boats careen across the stitches, etching out
each vein as it swells and subsides. Do you hear? Can you

restore it with your scent? Are my steps numbered?
Pulverized, you become a gift to yourself. I howl. Wholly
yours, Yellow Serpent. Titmouse. A cover. A bellows. A

wire. White-hot. I rule because your blood has destroyed
me. There is no death, no silence. This fist opening floods
and scalds everything. Your bulk collapses in a torrent.

To Edvard Kocbek on his 70th Birthday

I have avoided you, great poet
and thinker, you were too heavy
a burden. I drew a fierce line behind me
so that I would be at ease, light,

agile. A tiny mote of sunlight,
dancing as it crunches the muses' host
for a joke, as it spits the seeds of every orange
high in the air. You were

powerful, not an orange. How
they glint, how they shine, so that children
point at the colorful kites riding on the wind. I was
the oblivious apple tree which had

watered its soil. Today I know
who, more than anyone, is the shaper
of our freedom. And I am shaken,
I quickly raise my glass

to your health. You see, precisely
because this is a holiday I must
continue crunching. Moment
by moment joy strengthens.

1974

Walled in Alive

Communists use the same chairs, the same
stairways. There's blood flowing under their skin,
too. When they eat, they swallow. They look with their eyes,
their houses are hooked up to the same electric

current. For many years I had a communist for
a best friend. And my own
children: frightening examples of half communists, half
people. They're scattered. With communists it's always

either/or, and because they didn't liquidate
me at their height, they've missed their chance. Still
they retain all power and control, the clocks,
the bells, they can still tell your child

in broad daylight to his face, "Join us,
be a communist." They have mouths like ants
and do not reject property. They've been riveted
to the Central Committee building with nails. Walled

up in the corridors of power they call
innermost. Even though there's greenery all around,
even though there are plenty of trees all around, in the city's
center. Communists are a precise blow to

the blood. Their dew is inhaled invisibly.
And they go to their graves in peace, to music,
forever. Sad and shaken, as though
this were the same sort of death as ours.

1986

Rattenau

That in a spell you would undress again,
cover your head, waiting for me.
That your limbs would be round and soft as a magnet.
That you'd be hungry, not contrived.
Nailed down in sweat, but hungry for more.
That you'd rush to me as I rush to you.
You, who set me on fire.
You, who suck me, charge me, empty me.
When I caress you, your forests rustle.
You flame up in my protection.
Deadly is my love.
I fear I'll spring out like a cannon.
Like a fish's eye.
That I'll get sucked into you, feed you like a battery.
Be to you a sojourn, and then dead.
Sing! Explore! Be obsessed by me again!
You didn't believe, didn't believe.
All the rocks you decanted.
And how much light you then spilled out!
You cut your little hairs, they grew
while you were writing a bible.
How you let me smell you!
How you let me caress you!
How your voice tightened—
as sucked to sweetness—
when I called you from far away.
You were aroused. Hot. Kind and soft as
bread. Silken and giving.
The place you walked on thundered.
We drank. I pastured my soul,
you bound it. And then we merged
together like two soft raggedy dolls,
wringing ourselves out like prince Marko

with his sheepskin coat, which had been drying for ages—
and he wrung out one drop.
When you fell you didn't get hurt.
You grasped me. Shaved my head.
Enveloped in our breathing we were
lying down, listening.
You embedded but a little.
O silk! Struggle! Clock! Dark blue hive!
I remodeled all your hard rocks into
a soft bulk, building. You pushed me away
gently, saying: don't be
crazy. You are too crazy. And
covered me when I was cooling down.
Hugging me even when you wanted to read.
I pastured myself as if buried in clover.
Your hardness was so soft I
awoke more youthful.
Will you ever sail out of my soul, you, the gentle?
Now I am your rock.
Chained down.

Snakeskin, Samurai's Eye

Do you see what you really like: the rims.
Squeezing, pinching until blood runs.
The dust that grabs you and hardens your look.
You want to be more than power.

You called me and encrusted me.
I'm pulsing. The red-hot heart under
the grey membrane of the kasha.
Under your mechanical genre.
Under your halls and disgust.

O ore, you don't burn out your pain anymore.
I'm rubbing the fruit into you, O terrible,
confining and governing the blood of your virgins.
But you won't give up. You won't give up.
You know you're falling in love with me.

Outline and Eternity

Death link. Pisces with cancer.
White mouth. A circle, a circle gleams.
Nibs. Poles. Mallet.
Moans of the crowd. Silent running.

A stream of grains carries off the weeds.
The créche is watered. The créche is watered.
The soft edge is stretched and watered.
Colors and forms of density.

They brush and caress, soften and subdue.
Every joint, every plank connects.
The past rumbles, rushes into

the granary. The wheat's at home. The work
is caressing. A trembling. An offering.
Honey. And not one drop flows away.

[untitled]

I long for solid earth in heaven,
to lick your eyelids and stay even.
So they do not rise.

Earth

Koper defines darkness. Mothballs of circumcision
go to Cannes. Say you traveled under and over the earth,
returning like stitches. I didn't. The engineer

leveled my swim across his drawing board. Water!
My yellow Ami boiled over. The same with the homeopath
questioning the spawner: he can't

hope for the truth. The meetings were always
the previous ones. When they bring shrouds, compasses,
bibs—did you add something to the signature? You

don't know if moss drips from your tongue. There are
submissions. Trees tied together like braids
that rub together. A guarantee is a long hair. Small

is the body, huge the fin, and what you call
brutality: self-evident. Touch this
landscape beneath her. I don't want to watch

them torture pancakes. They're lusty. You
are all lusty. They all anoint the circle of the sun.
Virgins, foam, fish. We leap over her

along with density. Between the first breath and
the second the sex veers, it wants every fruit.
Violence tears water apart and plucks lint. The miracle

keeps occurring. When the wood pile before
the mountain cabin is torn down, and a cricket,
a fugue, and a *cantilena* are the same: utter bliss.

Wounds

I'm scared.
I'm just a stone's throw away from God.
He caresses my nostrils, I know it, caresses me like cocaine.
He's red as a carpet of dawn.
I grab the entrails, too.
Smoke dissolves, soft, greasy.
I turn like a pail.
I am turning in a wheelchair
in the four directions of the world, like Mark's mother.
She's Chinese. The fields were reaped. The trees are
toxic.

Those taverns where the owner stands by the door,
hands in his pockets—sawdust on the floor—and whistles,
do they still exist?
The Knight, for example.
In geologic time the mountains here in San Francisco are old.
They're the youngest. On the altars, as though they have a little
dynamo, Mark's mother, the Chinese, is turning
like a compass. Pages from the book—they're torn out
by skates. So goes the day: if I
were eating handfuls of oats I would not feel anything.
I would not even know I was eating.

Cover me.
Cover me with a hood, grass, sand, rams, keep squeezing
the air out to prevent a tragedy.
Let me feel the beetles on my skin, let me feel them.
Let each of my hairs grow long enough
to hold a movie theater—and fog.
Then no one can see who's in there.

Let people make love under the screen,

let each stroke be blunt.
The dice, there's still time, let them evaporate.
Don't let the husks crack.
Let the husks crack.
The shells have silk in their teeth.
In the caves there are cableways, in the cableways
there are dwarves. Do you remember? If not
for your juices I would have evaporated long ago.
You shot me in the forehead.
You sang lullabies of No.

Everything entangled in corn hair rises.
The smoke—the smell calms us down.
You, too, are transparent clay.
An oak tree burns under the pumps.
I seize the iron U on the pier
and draw myself to the shore.
Sun, O my sun,
you're burning me.
If I lose You, I lose Form.

Versailles

The borders of the countries on the earth's crust
hold less than the frostwork on my window. The tree
gets dressed. Breaks. You whisper and splash with ice.
I hug you and brush you. I remove your teeth,

like piano keys, then put them in again. Now you are
different: evolution has leveled the trauma.
They will bite again and flash, they'll rob you
of your sadness. I'll blow you up and pop you again

and again, don't worry, I won't get tired. The skin
needs care and bait. And sometimes you have twelve floors
and we have to figure out immediately if you're a match.

To cut deeper and deeper into your taste. And also: to gently
herd them back, the pedestrians who tumbled out of your wing
at the silliest hour. You are Slovenian, therefore sad.

Riva

Fishermen's nets hang from the mouths of giants,
your eyes, flamingo, and your grey full-breasted flank.
Cranes are robbing steamers. At the top

of the gangway: "To your berths!" Cows' feet hang
like the broken teeth of a comb. Sparks erupt. Waiters
pin diamonds to the tablecloths, and at Hvar,

in front of the movie theater, someone's begging
to return the wallet I lost. Dikan got
to Vera. I took Branko's sister. Years later,

when we were smoking Kents: "When will you graduate?"
When I graduate I'll travel around the world. The blacks
hurled the junkie from the deck because he

urinated. He didn't lift the broom. You fought
with your grandfather. You couldn't
write. You survived because of the cold weather. You're used

to walking on ice. On Crete your skin blisters,
on huge grey stones still warm in December. Doctor
Jamnicki is coming back. If a hen is tied up

as a chick it will stay tied up. Nurses won't bite her.
During the night she walks with a jug on her
head, on the parquet floor. No paintings in our house.

The walls are round. Your hair is horsehair. *Che xe
viniù da vicin, anche te ga crollà tutta tua roba sporca. Mi?
Chi te ga crollà?* And the anxiety of lifting the lid

of the piano, the flash of the eyes. The procession

at the feast of Corpus Christi, huge bicycles
on the rafts. Jeti rides logs in the chute. Ashbery

at Cooper Union, 1986: "And if you did/good that's
fine, but if you did bad it don't make no
difference, you're equal/same as the others,

and the devil don't give a shit who you are or
whether your name has an umlaut to it." *Flow Chart*,
Carcanet, pg. 100. That's why you can't manage *cavallotti*.

And spitting and joking, *no te capisci chi voga.*
Pretty, but she doesn't dress well. Little balls,
seething beads, they swallow them for the little one.

*Mákar, kaić, tu Dio che sii Stabile. Meglio un succo di
pompelmo.* And then again Hermes in Olympia, stolen
pajamas on the boat in Pirius. Throw yourself on the needles.

Isolani; pescecani. No way. No way at all, not
even if you want to. Who will get the milk? You've already got
the lederhosen. *Ma Dio, chi xe viniù sta sera. Dai,*

dai, butta xo ciapin. Did Hera avenge him
with fried polenta? Mozart wasn't shy,
he didn't stop staring. We kill English

kings. We're feeding the cartridge clips. Lynda's father
laundered money for the Mafia. She's walking with her pillow,
writing *Ghost Money*. The humble one, the silent

chicken is swallowing cubic meters of the sublime.
The thing is, parents have to limp. Or tell them
you were crawling over emptiness. Over everything white.

Everything in drizzle. Everything in the snowbound forest

tied to the Mediterranean. At the second lake, yes, I heard,
at the composers' hut—last year he was bitten

by the tsetse fly, he didn't come back from Africa.
The same one who said you have to splatter
your ego everywhere. I forget his name. I have

little crocodiles on my tongue, without a story.
Beetles are nibs. The secret addition
to human hair. You see, if death catches me, the white

mass will stay, pudding we'll fight over. Supply
is not the problem. What is it then? Flickering
lights in Janitio, an Oriental regard? Railroad tracks

crushed, arms ripped out. In the Venetian mirrors
they licked the connections. *No te xe vecio, te ghe diría,*
si, che te diría. Mai da un lado. The atmosphere

brought back the Breceljs and Beblers. The Bogomils
vanished and married. This is our jamboree. And
we won't pick any flowers, they're protected.

Lacquer

Destiny rolls over me. Sometimes like an egg. Sometimes
with its paws, slamming me into the slope. I shout. I take
my stand. I pledge all my juices. I shouldn't
do this. Destiny can snuff me out, I feel it now.

If destiny doesn't blow on our souls, we freeze
instantly. I spent days and days afraid
the sun wouldn't rise. That this was my last day.
I felt light sliding from my hands, and if I didn't

have enough quarters in my pocket, and Metka's voice
were not sweet enough and kind and solid and
real, my soul would escape from my body, as one day

it will. With death you have to be kind.
Home is where we're from. Everything in a moist dumpling.
We live only for a flash. Until the lacquer dries.

Who's Standing

Are you the stone of a fruit, dear soul? Mandorla, fetus
in white coffee? Your eyes are flames,
the dark grains of my ladies.
Shut the slot if you can't watch it.
Take a break.
My love is a holdup lifting you slowly,
slowly, so the air doesn't run out.
The tears you never confessed to fell
into soup bowls, in a Slovenian
village inn. The shawl was
green, red, from Kashmir.
We lost it then.
But you are a cube in me,
little light burning endlessly on the grave.

I watched the ascent, the food,
your blood pulsing on different continents.
Tunnels in parallel worlds
collapsing.
In the fire we saved
the sizzle of your tennis shoes. I pasted you up
with resin, with tokens, so you could breathe
only through your rhomboids.
I shoed you or
cleared the sky when I
starved you, when I taped up
your gargling.

How much longer will I be cut into pieces?
Loaded among wooden logs.

The Dromedary from the Altar at Ghent

Ride your bike to Cordoba! Your rain
will be my rain. I am the rain, little
tiger, you'll rave steam as you ride over puddles,

and south of Lille I'll overthrow you.
Your knee will be scraped, your blood will
run. Do you remember chasing me at Glinščica

(in dry summer), overestimating my bones
and dreaming I would fail (I was dreaming) and,
to complete the picture, smash into the rocks.

I can't hurry across the screes in the waterfall
that smells of moss. And Pavle pressed him to fish out
a hundred lira, and you scolded me for talking

to the little girl. You were melting, I wasn't.
I needed a moment for her to alloy my heart. Unglue
and paste your sandals. Ride your bike to Cordoba!

I'm a pumpkin. I'm standing in the middle of the heart.
My limbs are Europe's pair of compasses. I've made myself
as soft as the bread in Lisbon. Do you remember

how you shouted ten times in Ghent—without
feeling a thing. Smilja is blindfolding the crabs
so they'll mate faster. Drink beer (Blanche) and dance!

In Antwerp, at the Stagecoach

You escaped again!
What crunches is not God.
O long window of the cathedral,
ray of cardboard, Fontana Trevi,
the knife is shining, the sweetness.

Kalamazoo!
Curved lips of the Pygmies,
tanks, covered with frogs' beards,
wheels and steel against my face, I am
lying on the back in a double V,
in the membrane, in the nutritious membrane.

Touching the smooth surface, he snaps a picture of the frog.
My Lord is a circle.
I was calling you back when you climbed
the roof, when you dug in the leaves, in the cold.
Did you imagine you would soil the slippers?
We would be exposed.
So I only wore my hands away,
took them off, hung them on you
and spun you like a top.

The salad was creaking in the dustbins.
You were the thread of the orchestra sewn
in paradise, when the chestnuts cracked.

In Galilee, 1990

The skier puts barley on his head. Here, along
the Thames, Dickens lived. No lust bigger than that
in the province, in the small town where your grandfather

planted chestnut trees, you're building an opera house.
Endless personnel discussions. Who should
sing, who's on the schedule. Madame Nastja, night

and day—she spends her life phoning and cabling.
But here in Guanajuato we're spoiled. We have
another town, two, three hundred meters

underground, with rivers and cathedrals and silver
mines. Our mummies do not rot. Caruso loses
two pounds every time he sings. He drinks

magnesium, he smells. There are merchants in the garden
waiting with their parcels, displaying hats. Tzilka
seats them on the banks. No man, no majordomo,

outdoors, as if we were in Haloze. And when you extend
the park, on the other side you come across
the planks. Not like Coyoacan. There the walls

are high. You can't see much from outside. You hardly
hear the blow of the ice pick meant for Trotsky,
and yet his lower jaw was inherited

by Vera. Vasko and I are watching her. The merchants'
parcels got soaked. The singers will not sing.
Never again will the does wander away from the castle.

Photograph with a Quote from Yazoo: Deep in Each Other's Dream

Christ is my sex object, therefore I am
not an ethical problem. I lead him to the meadows.
Like a little shepherd, I force him to graze.

I root him out and clean his glands. Shall we
rinse ourselves under the tree? And when
we stretch out on the earth and watch the sky,

what moves? Will we have enough heat
for winter? Will we peel potatoes? Will
we make soldiers out of molten lead? Are we

going to the cows with our arms in their muzzles?
Will we bite the horsetail? Watch Mount Nanos.
We'll hide in the moss, under sheets of glass.

When you took the picture of the tree, did you
take care of the explosion? What do you mean exactly?
The white milk traveling through the veins

into eternity, glazing the dark? I am a little stone
falling into your flesh. I made you twitch
and tied you up. We crucified you.

Ambergris

I was in the place where ambergris collects.
The word is dark, we do not see anything in it.
Oak leaves climb out of a mouth, we lift up

buckets from the sinking ships. The whiteness
of chilblains of my goods. Fields of white silk. I am
in thick steel, in the rustling bedspring, in the cube,

which is just beginning to sculpt the figure.
The wind in the jasmine doesn't see any decanting.
As I will fall. What are hands if breasts are

heavier? I'm walking on the nails. Ocean liners sip
cookies. No little birds in this tableau. I walled
myself in with looks and gazes, I'm rolling. The soles

of little feet are skiing the warm arches of the brain.
And honor knows. I was standing with God, back to back,
in the white, solemn mass. The Mithraic temple is the scream.

I breathed on iron and it turned to fango.
The surface of the yarn, the surface of legumes,
it's thunder, *direi che sii bravo*, knock, knock. Don't

jump, stay back. Visits open up the vaults of witnesses.
You'll see the eye of the colonnade, fat and boiling.
The long distance running of your own face.

Bridges will be shackled. Huge links of the chain,
the bridge will be the bonbon. Hinds and blossoms
will spurt up with their little noses and brothers.

Beauty will lie down. You'll poke holes in it.

So it won't harden. So pyrites and basalt
and the Indians in Puebla will stay on the shelves.

They'll exchange little hoops and crosses and
knock on the necks of roosters. In the drawing
room it will flutter. The second sentence

belongs to Evgen Bavčar. Nobody spent
a sleepless night in Bohinj. We noble lords, we
let you take everything off here. To let you make a thesaurus.

Mishkenot Sha'ananim

The beak is scrubbing.
The map melts the windowpane.
Who's stepping straight into the prey?
Are cakes born?
Who keeps me from having a head like agave
and chakra full of saliva?
From being a model for India?

So that Raj Raj would
watch me, as if I were burning
the body of my dead father
and watching the crackling juices,
noting them down.
Hindus can eat you like
flour without even

touching you.
They do not go like scales into the soul.
Their gaze is fleshlike.
Not sexual but full of
the flesh of lotus water.
Raj Raj's grandfather was already
a professor in Chicago.

The Brahmin is water. The Chinese
is a butterfly. No Chinese
described for me how he burned
his father. The Chinese are
moths, and they are not talking.
They remind me of pumps in a lab,
of green birds. The white man,

I can peel him, corrode him, tie him up.

I can stuff him with memories so that on his
deathbed, like a reliable clock, he will
cry out. But if
the Brahmin imagines your body on the pyre
licked by flames, he wants

to be friends.
You are for him the infinite
possibility. I am zipping up the tent
of my heaven. I am a white flame,
a shadow through the linen, but in fact
heavy and gluttonous as a newborn
Buddha, a Pantagruel.

The Walk

My stone is ribs. They're flattening out and they
breathe. He takes me in his mouth, praying
for me. The Lord will flow all over me. Like sugar
He will moisten your heart, watch you,
brush you. Like a horse, like a stallion. O
my sugary colossus, my heart in You. Do you hear
how the little wet hair pulses in the hall? Look: it roars
from the choir but you're licking your lips at the studs
in the hardware store. I've taken you with a veto.
I'm guarding you. You're rinsed with the scent
of silent walks when the pine trees waken.
You stroll with your dog above the Sava River,
thinking, unattached, free. The corpses of God's flesh
pour down your throat, and you clean them. Thank you.

Johannes

Who opens the nose of the compost? Pranajama
in the coccyx. A little cement wall for the compost,
under the lilac bush, behind the walnut tree.

All leveled now by bulldozers. This is the little wall
where I used to watch Pika before her lungs
dried up. Or else she died in the fire

because her fragments collapsed. Maybe she saw me
on the little wall, watching her come home
from a walk. Her flesh started to peel, her brains

spilled out, maybe a bitch ate them.
Anyway she died, four or five years old,
because I watched her from that little wall.

She was approximately three months
younger than Katka, and buried very young. Pika's
corpse confused me. I am watering, with buckets,

the orange trees. Then I take cream and draw
a ring around all the oppressed. I am making a magic
circle, putting it to the test, especially

the permeability of its walls. When I fortify
it, I widen it and make it stronger, to pierce
the strengthened one. When you pierce

the magic circle it makes a hole in the material
like a bullet traveling through the sole
of a foot eight inches thick. A soul

has little chance of looking from the outside

in again. But if you try really hard,
maybe in Quechuan, a language

pressed in a red or a brown tunnel for you
to take home to remember. The amulet dries up.
Mercury gives it water. And it blows

and smacks its lips like a locomotive
which wants to uproot itself from the rails.
It ends up hanging in the woods, among

tree trunks, in the shadows, in a quiet
soothing Baltic grove, on the moss
where Bobrowski used to rest.

Kiss the Eyes of Peace

Kiss the eyes of Peace, may it stream down
upon the trees. The sun shines and no longer roars
so intolerably. The soul again hopes to sense its
ribs, the sap. The cold has done me good. If the wind
blows, and I walk and watch the cars, life
brings me back to itself. It would be terrible
not to recognize anyone at the departure.
They'd be too far to touch or
be felt. In the pitch darkness I would not hold the memory
of love. A crust of ice forms on molten lava.
In time I might again be able to slide off. Walk
those roads of dust. Shake the jacket off, if it's
dusty. There has been too much honey and grace, that's
all. Too many blessings break a man apart.

Index of Poems and Translators

About the Poet

Tomaž Šalamun was born in Zagreb, Croatia and raised in Koper, Slovenia. A graduate in art history from the University of Ljubljana, he worked as a conceptual artist before devoting his energy to poetry. Widely recognized as one of the leading Central European poets, he is the author of twenty-five collections of poetry, and his books have been translated into many languages. His honors include the Mladost Prize, the Prešeren Fund Prize, the Jenko Prize, a fellowship to the International Writing Program at the University of Iowa, residencies at Yaddo and the McDowell Colony, a visiting Fulbright to Columbia University, and a Pushcart Prize. Married to the painter Metka Krašovec, he is the father of two grown children, Ana and David. Šalamun, who is Cultural Attaché for the Republic of Slovenia, divides his time between New York City and Ljubljana.

About the Editor

Christopher Merrill is the author of ten books, including three collections of poetry, *Workbook, Fevers & Tides,* and *Watch Fire;* a translation of Aleš Debeljak's *Anxious Moments;* and two works of nonfiction, *The Grass of Another Country: A Journey Through the World of Soccer* and *The Old Bridge: The Third Balkan War and the Age of the Refugee.* He holds the Jenks Chair in Contemporary Letters at the College of the Holy Cross. He and his wife, violinist Lisa Gowdy-Merrill, are the parents of a daughter, Hannah.

Poetry in Translation from White Pine Press

THE FOUR QUESTIONS OF MELANCHOLY
Tomaz Salamun
224 pages $15.00 paper

THESE ARE NOT SWEET GIRLS
An Anthology of Poetry by Latin American Women
320 pages $17.00 paper

A GABRIELA MISTRAL READER
277 pages $13.00 paper

ALFONSINA STORNI: SELECTED POEMS
72 pages $8.00 paper

CIRCLES OF MADNESS: MOTHERS OF THE PLAZA DE MAYO
Marjorie Agosín
128 pages $13.00 paper   Bilingual

SARGASSO
Marjorie Agosín
92 pages $12.00 paper   Bilingual

MAREMOTO/SEAQUAKE
Pablo Neruda
64 pages $9.00 paper   Bilingual

THE STONES OF CHILE
Pablo Neruda
98 pages $10.00 paper   Bilingual

VERTICAL POETRY: RECENT POEMS BY ROBERTO JUARROZ
118 pages $11.00 paper   Bilingual

LIGHT AND SHADOWS
Juan Ramon Jimenez
70 pages $9.00 paper

ELEMENTAL POEMS
Tommy Olofsson
70 pages $9.00 paper

FOUR SWEDISH POETS:
STROM, ESPMARK, TRANSTROMER, SJOGREN
131 pages $9.00 paper

NIGHT OPEN
Rolf Jacobsen
221 pages $15.00 paper

SELECTED POEMS OF OLAV HAUGE
92 pages $9.00 paper

TANGLED HAIR
Love Poems of Yosano Akiko
48 pages $7.50 paper Illustrated

A DRIFTING BOAT
An Anthology of Chinese Zen Poetry
200 pages $15.00 paper

BETWEEN THE FLOATING MIST
Poems of Ryokan
88 pages $12.00 paper

WINE OF ENDLESS LIFE
Taoist Drinking Songs
60 pages $9.00 paper

TANTRIC POETRY OF KUKAI
80 pages $7.00 paper

American Poetry from White Pine Press

BODILY COURSE
Deborah Gorlin
90 pages $12.00 paper
Winner 1996 White Pine Press Poetry Prize

TREEHOUSE: NEW & SELECTED POEMS
William Kloefkorn
224 pages $15.00 paper

CERTAINTY
David Romtvedt
96 pages $12.00 paper

ZOO & CATHEDRAL
Nancy Johnson
80 pages $12.00 paper
Winner 1995 White Pine Press Poetry Prize

DESTINATION ZERO
Sam Hamill
184 pages $15.00 paper
184 pages $25.00 cloth

CLANS OF MANY NATIONS
Peter Blue Cloud
128 pages $14.00 paper

HEARTBEAT GEOGRAPHY
John Brandi
256 pages $15.00 paper

LEAVING EGYPT
Gene Zeiger
80 pages $12.00 paper

WATCH FIRE
Christopher Merrill
192 pages $14.00 paper

BETWEEN TWO RIVERS
Maurice Kenny
168 pages $12.00 paper

TEKONWATONTI: MOLLY BRANT
Maurice Kenny
209 pages $12.00 paper

DRINKING THE TIN CUP DRY
William Kloefkorn
87 pages $8.00 paper

GOING OUT, COMING BACK
William Kloefkorn
96 pages $11.00 paper

JUMPING OUT OF BED
Robert Bly
48 pages $7.00 paper

POETRY: ECOLOGY OF THE SOUL
Joel Oppenheimer
114 pages $7.50 paper

WHY NOT
Joel Oppenheimer
46 pages $7.00 paper

TWO CITIZENS
James Wright
48 pages $8.00 paper

SLEEK FOR THE LONG FLIGHT
William Matthews
80 pages $8.00 paper

WHY I CAME TO JUDEVINE
David Budbill
72 pages $7.00 paper

AZUBAH NYE
Lyle Glazier
56 pages $7.00 paper

SMELL OF EARTH AND CLAY
East Greenland Eskimo Songs
38 pages $5.00 paper

FINE CHINA: TWENTY YEARS OF EARTH'S DAUGHTERS
230 pages $14.00 paper